Daniela Klein
LITTLE SWEETS AND BAKES

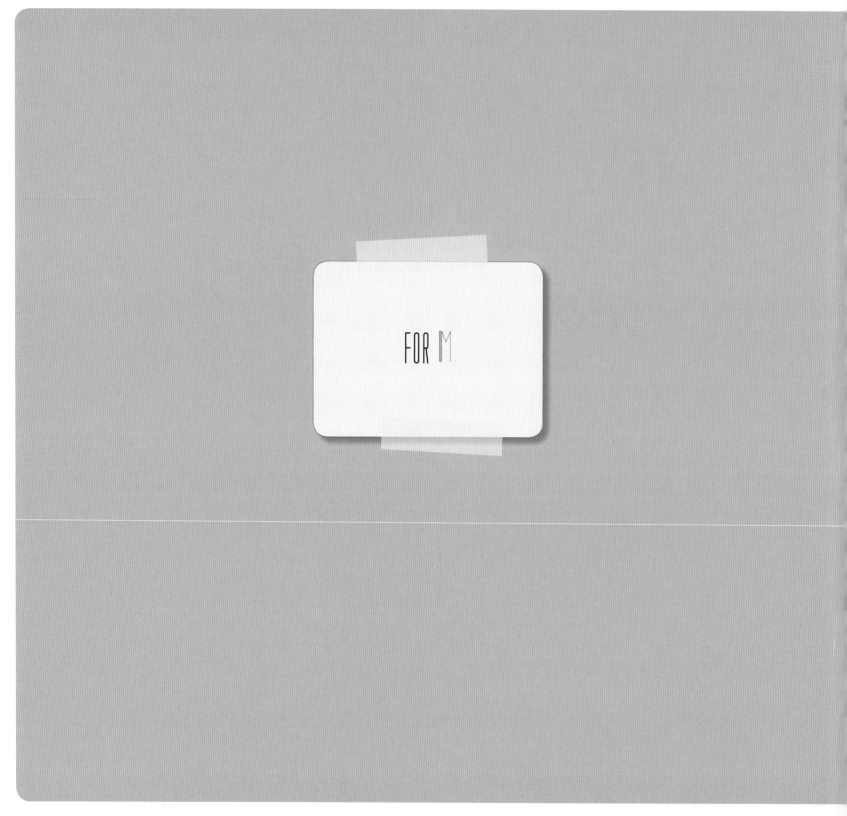

FOR M

Translation by Danae Bianes

Daniela Klein
LITTLE SWEETS AND BAKES

Easy-to-Make Cupcakes, Cake Pops, Whoopie Pies, Macarons, and Decorated Cookies

WITH PHOTOGRAPHS
FROM MR. K

SKYHORSE PUBLISHING

CONTENTS

FOREWORD

Sometimes the craziest things happen in life. Opportunities open up, which you had never expected to come to you. "Me, a cookbook author? Never!" I would have said to you a year ago. Naturally everyone is allowed to imagine the most amazing things are happening in their dreams, but to actually have that become a reality?

Perhaps I should have warned you I'm in a completely different career field that has nothing to do with baking or crafting. All of this is a passion of mine I've enjoyed sharing on my klitzekleine blog for the last two years with like-minded souls.

You are holding in your hands the documentation of that. A book, filled to the brim with little sweets and bakes to make you happy. Things I discovered somewhere along the way and that have surprised me. A list of creations that were buzzing around in my head and recipes from great bloggers and friends. Packaging ideas that were implemented with much love. And of course the "All-Time Favorites" with which the Klein household could never think of doing away.

How did you stumble upon *Little Sweets and Bakes*? Do you also enjoy eating cheese-cake like my father, or do you tend to read cookbooks before going to bed like me? Is baking your passion? Will you give this book to a good friend because she has a big sweet tooth like you?

I make a very polite curtsy, and wish you lots of joy while you browse and bake. Merci, merci, and thank you.

A FEW FACTS
ABOUT ME

I sleep with woolen socks on in the middle of summer. I seldom keep up with a hobby for more than a year - guitar, piano, and flute have remained by the wayside. I use a calculator to figure out 13-8. You could kill me with tartar.

Above all else I like black and white and every now and then bright colors. My biggest weakness? Being impatient.

I'm no baker, graphic designer, photographer, artist, or journalist. Everything here and on my blog was made and tested by me. I never get enough of pretty pictures. Since Pinterest I can collect them without my hard drive struggling along in the process.

My favorite number is 18. Once a month I get a new business idea - it is never used. My greatest joy is to make others happy - especially when it comes unexpectedly. I am extremely messy - but I'd like to think it all depends on one's perspective. Currently I prefer to wear my hair in a ponytail, because Herr K. says, "With that haircut you look 35!" He can tell me that again when I'm 40. Herr K. = big love.

Fresh bread, cheese, milk, honey? My staple groceries. Athletic? I was once. The garden will never be rid of me. I own a maximum of 8 CDs, though more like 6. Herr K. owns infinitely more. My last wish is to go to Sweden. *At least I shared that with the anesthesiologist right before my tonsillectomy.

Before I take on a challenge, I Google it until my fingers are sore. Clothes and make-up empty out my wallet on a monthly basis. If I watch a scary movie I can't sleep for a whole year! I have avoided them since I was 12 years old.

Astrid Lindgren, picking blueberries and fishing with Papa, arts and crafts, pottery, baking, cooking and painting with Mama, bickering with and tolerating my little sister, my hamster Max, vacations with grandma and my cousins at the camping grounds are all my childhood. My family and my friends are deep within my heart and know my quirks - but love me anyway, and that makes me smile at least once every day.

www.klitzeklein.wordpress.com

CHOCOLATE

VANILLA

ESSENTIAL RECIPES & TIPS

CAKE POPS

MAKES 30-35

Stylish snacking is the theme here. A chocolate cake on a stick makes quite the stir. They will hardly be served before dessert lovers pull out their recipe notebooks to write it down. "How did you make that?" or "Is it complicated?" and "Could I make that, too?" Of course. It's really very simple. All you need is a little time. But these tiny calorie bombs are worth the utmost effort. I promise!

Sponge cake: 1 chocolate, vanilla, or red velvet cake ⟹ Pages 14/15

Cream: 1/4 cup (60 g) butter (room temperature)   1 teaspoon vanilla extract ⟹141   1 cup (120 g) powdered sugar   1 tablespoon milk

Glaze: 2 1/2 cup (600 g) fondant icing, Candy Melts or Callebaut Callets ⟹ 140

Also: 1 skewer   Styrofoam block 12 in × 20 in × 4 in (30 cm × 50 cm × 10 cm) ⟹ 140   35 lollipop sticks ⟹ 141

1. Prepare a sponge cake following the recipe (⟹ 14/15) and let it cool completely. Cut off the crust around the edges and carefully crumble the cake with your hands. There should not be any large pieces left.

2. To make the cream, stir the butter and vanilla extract in a bowl to a creamy texture. Sift the powdered sugar and stir it into the mix little by little. Add in the milk and mix everything well. Thoroughly knead the cream with the cake crumbles. The mix should be relatively moist so that while forming the balls they will not fall apart.

3. Form small balls out of the finished dough (you can make cylinders, mushrooms, cupcakes, donuts or cubes as well). Pay close attention because the cake balls will become subsequently bigger after being glazed; so hold back a bit when shaping them out of the dough. Later, the cake pop should only be as big as it should take you to make it disappear in two bites. Leave the finished balls in the refrigerator for approximately 10—15 minutes.

4. Because the cake pops will be put in a Styrofoam block to dry, punch 35 holes into the Styrofoam with a skewer. Melt the glaze for 1—2 minutes in the microwave or in a water bath (⇒15) and fill the deepest possible bowl so that you can dip the cake balls easily.

5. Push the pointy end of the lollipop sticks about 1/3 in (1 cm) deep into the glaze and then poke the sticks directly into the cake balls a little more than halfway through. Now the balls cannot slide as quickly off of the sticks.

6. If the glaze has dried on somewhat, dip the whole ball into the glaze and wait until the excess drains away. To dry place the cake balls in the Styrofoam block. In case the glaze is not totally covering the cake ball, you can repeat the process again. The cake pops can be decorated to your heart's desire.

SPONGE CAKES AND GLAZES FOR CAKE POPS

When I'm in a hurry, I allow myself to use a ready-made baking mix for the sponge cakes. For all intents and purposes it works just as well. However, the cake pops do taste better if you make the dough by hand. Here are my three all-time favorites . . .

RED VELVET CAKE

....

Dough: 1 cup 1 1/2 tablespoon (250 g) butter (room temperature)   1 cup (200 g) sugar   1 teaspoon vanilla extract ⇨ 141   4 eggs   3 tablespoons milk   1 1/2 cup 1 1/2 tablespoon (200 g) flour   3/4 cup 1/2 tablespoon (100 g) starch   1 packet baking powder   1 tablespoon cocoa powder   1 teaspoon red food coloring ⇨ 141   1 pinch of salt   Butter and flour for the pan

Materials: 1 box-shaped baking pan 10 in (26 cm)

....

1. Set the oven to 350 °F (175 °C) on the baking setting to preheat. Grease the pan and sprinkle lightly with flour. Mix the butter, sugar, and vanilla extract to a creamy texture. Separate the eggs. Add the milk and then the egg yolks to the butter. Stir well. Mix the flour, starch, baking powder, and cocoa powder together in another bowl and little by little add to the butter. Whip the egg whites with the red food coloring and salt. Gently fold into the batter.

2. Fill the pan with the dough and smooth the top portion so that it is flat. Bake for 60 minutes in the oven. For the best results test the cake with a toothpick, that way nothing can go wrong. Let the cake cool for 10 minutes before removing from the pan and placing on a cooling rack. If the cake does not yet have the desired color, you can add more red food coloring while making the cake balls.

CHOCOLATE CAKE

....

Dough:

3/4 cup 2 tablespoon (200 g) butter (room temperature)

1 1/4 cup (250 g) sugar

1 packet of vanilla sugar

Essence of rum (as desired)

3 eggs

2 1/2 cup 2 tablespoon (330 g) flour

1 packet baking powder

3 tablespoons cocoa powder

3/4 cup 3 tablespoon (225 ml) milk

Butter and flour for the pan

Materials:

1 box-shaped baking pan 10 in (26 cm)

1. Preheat the oven to 350 °F (175 °C) on the baking setting. Grease the pan and sprinkle lightly with flour. Mix the butter, sugar, vanilla sugar (and as desired the essence of rum) in a bowl to a creamy texture. Add the eggs one by one and work them into the mixture. Mix the flour, baking powder, and cocoa together and alternately add in the milk. Stir well.

2. Fill the pan with the dough, smooth flat, and bake in the oven for around 60 minutes. Conduct the toothpick test, keep the finished cake in the pan for 10 minutes, remove and then let cool.

VANILLA CAKE

....

Dough:

1 cup 1 1/2 tablespoon (250 g) butter (room temperature)

1 cup (200 g) sugar

1 teaspoon vanilla extract ⟹ 141

4 eggs

3 tablespoons milk

1 1/2 cup 1 1/2 tablespoon (200 g) flour

3/4 cup 1/2 tablespoon (100 g) starch

1 packet baking powder

1 pinch of salt

Butter and flour for the pan

Materials:

1 box-shaped baking pan 10 in (26 cm)

1. Preheat the oven to 350 °F (175 °C) on the baking setting. Grease the pan and sprinkle lightly with flour. Mix the butter, sugar, and vanilla extract in a bowl to a creamy texture. Separate the eggs. Add the milk and then the egg yolks to the butter. Stir well. Mix the flour, starch, and baking powder together in another bowl and little by little add to the butter. Whip the egg whites with a pinch of salt until stiff and gently add into the batter.

2. Fill the pan with the dough, smooth flat, and bake in the oven for 60 minutes. Keep the finished cake in the pan for 10 minutes, remove and then let cool.

CAKE GLAZE

Allow the icing to melt on its own and spread onto the cake ball. It will have the perfect consistency and dries quickly. The only drawback is that the cake ball must be glazed twice. My favorite icing!

CANDY MELTS

Couverture chocolate is rather tricky to liquefy. Before melting I add 1—2 big tablespoons vegetable fat and continue stirring now and then. That prevents a bigger, unsalvageable clump from forming. Once that is done, the cake balls can be easily glazed. Here a layer of icing is sufficient. Candy melts dry just as quickly as icing.

CALLEBAUT CALLETS

Callebaut callets look like candy melts and need 1—2 tablespoons vegetable fat to melt as well. Here you must also continuously stir every now and then. The disadvantage: this icing has a very long drying time. ⟹ 140

MACARONS

MAKES 15-20

....

Dough: 1 cup 2 1/2 tablespoon (110 g) shelled & ground almonds   1 1/2 cup 2 1/2 tablespoon (200 g) powdered sugar   3 egg whites (90 g)
1 pinch of salt   2 1/2 tablespoon (30 g) sugar   1 pinch of food coloring of your preferred choice ⟹ 141

Cream: 1 cup 1 tablespoon (250 ml) milk   5 teaspoons flour   3/4 cup 2 tablespoon (200 g) butter (room temperature)   1 3/4 cup 2 tablespoon (225 g) powdered sugar   1 packet vanilla sugar   1 tablespoon powdered fruit of your preferred choice

....

1. Sift almonds with a fine strainer. Grind the almonds that don't pass through to an even finer quality with a chopping knife and run them back through the strainer. The powdered sugar should likewise be put through the strainer and mixed well with the almonds.

2. Next, take your 3 egg whites and beat in a bowl until very stiff. Sprinkle in a pinch of salt and the sugar. If desired, color the egg whites with food coloring. To do so, add the preferred color to the egg whites and carefully stir with a spatula until the entire quantity is equally colored throughout. Add the egg whites to the almond mix to create a dough and stir very gently so that the egg whites do not fall apart. The consistency should be similar to molten lava. Leave the mix to rest for about 2 minutes.

3. Lay a piece of parchment paper onto a baking sheet. Fill a pastry bag with the batter. You could also use a plastic bag by cutting off the corner. Squeeze the batter onto the paper in small dots leaving some distance between each dot on the sheet — to help, you can draw circles of 1 ¾—2 in (4—5 cm) on the baking paper with a food-grade crayon.

4. Leave the sheet out for 30 minutes before it goes into the oven. Thus, a thin layer of skin forms on the macarons so they do not melt during baking. Preheat the oven to 284 °F (140 °C) on the baking setting.

What is crunchy, tastes somewhat like marzipan, has a soft
core, and causes pure delight?
Macarons of course. When freshly
baked they are really irresist-
ible and photogenic on top of
that.

Thanks to Jenni, who has intro-
duced me to the world of macarons and gave me my first taste
of these tiny treats.

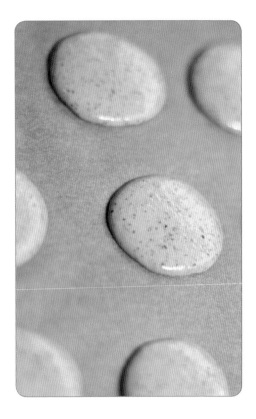

5. Bake the macaron halves for 12—15 minutes and let them cool down completely intact on the baking sheet. Afterward remove from baking paper. If the macarons aren't separating well from the paper, lightly moisten the work space and pull out the baking paper. Wait a short while and try again.

6. To make the cream, heat milk and flour in a saucepan while stirring until it reaches a pudding-like consistency. Stir this in a cold water bath. In another bowl, mix butter with the powered sugar and vanilla sugar. Stir well.

Now stir the milk and flour mixture into the butter until a homogeneous mass is formed and the sugar has completely dissolved. Add in fruit powder to taste.

7. Put the mix in the refrigerator for about 15 minutes so it becomes a little harder. Pour the butter cream into a pastry bag with a round tip or in a plastic bag with the tip cut off. Squirt a dab of butter cream onto half of a macaron and cover with another half.

FILLINGS

Macarons can be filled with ganache, fresh fruit, lemon curd, butter cream, jam, dulce de leche, praline cream or cream cheese. The stuffing keeps for 2—3 days depending on which kind is used, but they taste best fresh.

FAVORITE SUGAR COOKIES

MAKES 10-30 COOKIES, DEPENDING ON SIZE

The following is my favorite sugar cookie recipe. If the dough is processed IMMEDIATELY, the baked cookies taste sensational, just like vanilla shortbread. This recipe is perfect for the impatient baker. The sugar cookies also can be instantly turned into a cookie on a stick, pretty iced cookies you can hang as decoration, or colorful fondant cookies. This is a very multi-talented sugar cookie — imagination's the limit!

1 cup (230 g) butter (room temperature)
1 1/4 cup 2 tablespoon (165 g) powdered sugar
1 egg
½ teaspoon vanilla extract ⟹ 141
3 3.4 cup 1 tablespoon (475 g) flour
2 teaspoons baking powder
½ teaspoon salt
Flour for the work station

1. Preheat the oven to 400 °F (200 °C) on the baking setting and cover a baking sheet with parchment paper. Mix butter and powdered sugar until it is creamy. Whisk the egg together with the vanilla extract in a separate bowl and thoroughly add it into the butter and sugar mixture.

2. Mix the flour, baking powder, and salt together. Gradually add this to the butter and sugar mixture and knead with your hands into a firm dough. If the dough sticks to your fingers, you can still add a little flour. Let the dough rest for 2 minutes in the bowl.

3. Roll out the dough on the floured work station so that it is about ¼ in thick. Form dough into the desired shapes with cookie cutters and place on the baking sheet.

*Do you want to turn your sugar cookies into cookie pops? Then from here follow the instructions on page 19.

4. Bake the cookies in the oven for 7—8 minutes. Caution! The cookies should not brown. Let the finished cookies cool down on a wire rack completely intact. You can decorate them the next day. Thus you avoid the fat of the cookie getting into the glaze, absorbing the fondant and becoming discolored.

COOKIE POPS

HOW SUGAR COOKIES BECOME A COOKIE POP

You need: 20 oven-safe lollipop sticks ⟹ 141

Cookie Pops are cookies on a stick. Nothing more, but still very impressive. Any cookie shaped with cookie cutters is suitable for it. It is, however, very important that you use only oven-safe lollipop sticks.

1. Turn the cut, yet unbaked sugar cookies so that the bottom side is facing up and press the lollipop stick into the cookie.

2. Press some dough over the stem of the lollipop stick so that this will not separate from the cookie later on. Place the cookie with the bottom side down onto the baking paper.

3. Bake at 400 °F (200 °C) on the baking setting for 7—8 minutes in the oven. Please note that the cookies should not brown! Allow the finished cookies to cool on a wire rack. You can decorate them the next day. Thus you avoid the fat of the cookie getting into the glaze, absorbing the fondant and becoming discolored.

SUGARED ICING FOR THE COOKIES

PROCEDURE

There are two different ways to prepare the icing. The most well-known is the egg white glaze spray, to be used only with very fresh eggs. The other variant is the meringue frosting spray. The meringue spray or powder is not as common in Germany, but you can order it now (⟹ 141). I like both versions very much. The meringue powder version might be a little bit faster and a little fluffier than the egg white spray glaze. Bake the cookies a day before glazing them, because if the cookies are not really cold the fat will be absorbed into the icing and discolor the cookies. Now you can make either the egg white spray glaze or the glaze with the meringue powder.

Did you know that you need two different consistencies of icing to decorate a single cookie? I unfortunately learned through trial and error that you should first build a small border with a firmer glaze, and then the rest should be filled out with the thinner glaze.

ROYAL ICING WITH EGG WHITES MAKES 2 1/2 CUPS (600 G)

....

4 cup 2 1/2 tablespoon (500 g) powdered sugar   2 teaspoons fresh lemon juice   2 egg whites   food coloring as desired ⟹ 141
½ teaspoon baking extract (e.g. vanilla, lemon, almond)

....

Sift/strain the powdered sugar into a bowl. Add egg whites and lemon juice to the sugar and beat with an electric whisk for at least 6 minutes. The contents should now form stiff points sticking out.

ROYAL ICING WITH MERINGUE POWDER MAKES 2 2/3 CUPS (600 G)

3 1/2 cup 2 1/2 tablespoon (440 g) powdered sugar   3 tablespoon (30 g) meringue powder ⇒ 141   food coloring as desired ⇒ 141   ½ teaspoon baking extract (e.g. vanilla, lemon, or almond)

Strain/sift the powdered sugar into a bowl and gently stir in the meringue powder. Gradually add about 1/2 cup (120 ml) of lukewarm water and beat with a KitchenAid running at high speed for at least 6—7 minutes. If the contents are too dry, add some more water. It should now form stiff points. If not, add some more sifted powdered sugar. As desired, color and flavor the icing with food coloring. Keep the icing covered with plastic wrap until you work with it again. It will keep for at least 5 days in the refrigerator. Before working any further, beat the contents once more with the electric whisk.

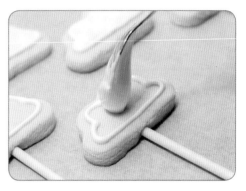

DILUTING

Here a little skill is needed! Since the edges don't need as much icing as the rest of the cookie, I put a small proportion of the glaze in a separate container and add water drop by drop. The consistency of the powdered sugar for the edges is close to that of toothpaste, while the consistency of the icing for the rest of the cookie is similar to shampoo. Between the two there are only a few drops of water difference. So always test the consistency. Do the same with the icing for the whole cookie. Stir in a few droplets of water until the consistency is achieved for glazing.

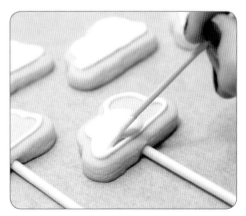

APPLICATION

What you need: pastry bag with a round tip and toothpicks. There we go! To glaze the cookies, take the firmer of the icings and fill a pastry bag to the brim, then close it with a rubber band so the glaze does not leak out of the top of the pastry bag. To get the edges glazed, hold the tip of the pastry bag diagonally a few millimeters over the cookies. The icing lining the edge should be completely closed, so that later no icing leaks out when it is filled. That alone already looks very nice. To coat the top of the cookies put a small dab of the liquid icing on the cookie and gently spread it out with a toothpick. Also, air bubbles can be removed wonderfully this way.

FONDANT CUPCAKES

MAKES 12

....

12 baked cupcakes as preferred (e.g. vanilla cupcakes ⟹ 78)

Pre-made butter cream to taste (e.g. vanilla cupcake cream ⟹ 78)

Fondant: 1 1/3 cup (300 g) fondant paste ⟹ 141   Food coloring as desired ⟹ 141

Also: Muffin tin   12 cupcake holders   Powdered sugar for the work space   Vegetable fat for your hands
Rolling pin ⟹ 141   Circular cookie cutters 2 1/2 in (6 1/2 cm)   Smoother ⟹ 141

....

Fondant cupcakes look simply delectable and are also not as complicated to make as it might look at first glance. If you've never worked with fondant, then they are the perfect way to start, plus they're a real eye-catcher on special occasions.

1. Make the cupcakes and butter cream according to the recipes. If the cupcakes fall apart while they are baking, cut with a sharp kitchen knife to reshape them after cooling a bit so that they can be easily decorated with fondant.

2. Coat the cupcakes with butter cream. Here it is best to use a small palette knife or a bread knife. Spread a thin layer of vanilla butter cream onto the cupcakes — up to the edge of the cupcake holder and in no case beyond it. Put on the flattest, most even layer possible, which can save you from needing to make corrections later on. Leave the cupcakes in the refrigerator for about 10 minutes, so that the butter cream gets a little harder.

3. Sprinkle the counter with powdered sugar. Grease your hands with some vegetable fat and knead the fondant well. Whoever wants to color the fondant can do so now. For the paste you often need less than a pinch of food coloring. A toothpick is wonderfully suited for dispensing the right amount. Roll out the fondant 2—3 mm thick and cut out a circle. Place the circle onto your outstretched hand, press the cupcake onto the fondant with the other hand. Using a fondant smoother helps to apply the fondant and keeps it smooth. When doing so, press quite firmly so

the fondant is distributed into every crack and adds the finishing touch to the perfect cupcake. The cupcakes can now be decorated as desired (e.g. windmill cupcakes [⟹ 38], birdie cupcakes [⟹ 116] or party cupcakes [⟹ 124]).

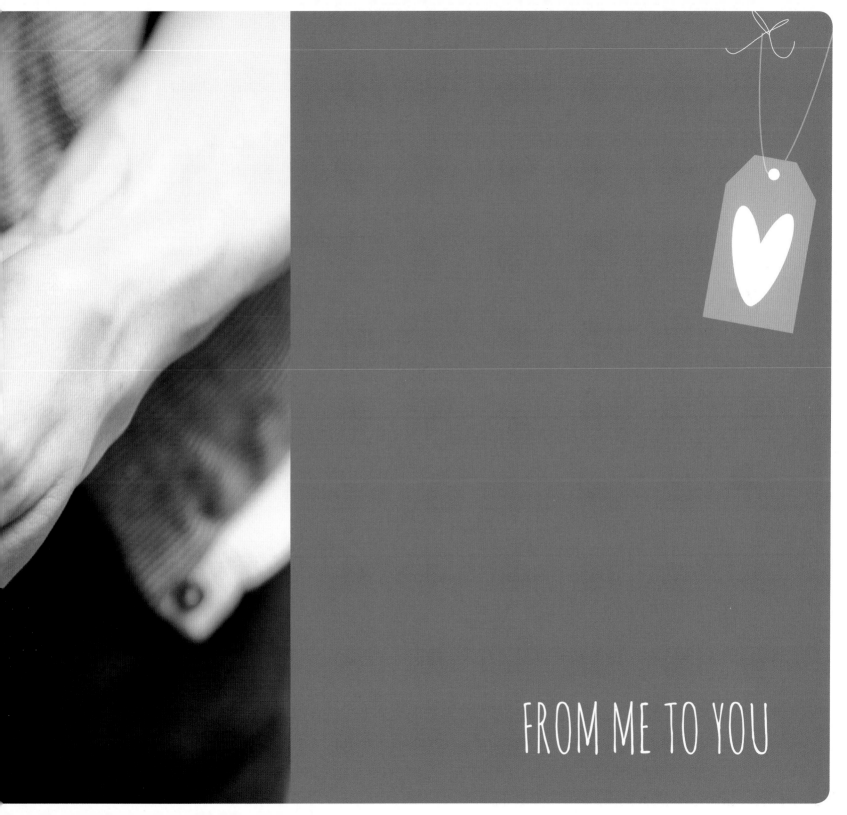

FROM ME TO YOU

PISTACHIO WHOOPIE PIES WITH ROSEWATER CREAM

MAKES 16

....

Dough: 1/2 cup (60 g) pistachios   1/2 cup 1 tablespoon (125 g) butter (room temperature)   3/4 cup 1 tablespoon (165 g) sugar   1 egg
1 teaspoon vanilla extract ⟹ 141   2 cup 1 tablespoon (260 g) flour   1 teaspoon baking powder   ½ teaspoon bicarbonate of soda
1/4 cup 2 1/2 tablespoon (100 ml) milk

Cream: 1 cup 2 1/2 tablespoon (260 g) butter (room temperature)   1 teaspoon vanilla extract ⟹ 141   3 cup 2 tablespoon (375 g) powdered
sugar
1 ½ teaspoon rose water ⟹ 141   1 pinch of pink food coloring ⟹ 141   Powdered sugar for dusting

Also: Pastry bag with a star tip ⟹ 141

....

1. For the whoopie pies preheat the oven to 360 °F (180 °C) on the baking setting. Cover two baking sheets with baking paper. Grind the pistachios and set aside in a food chopper. Mix the butter and sugar until creamy. Mix in the egg and vanilla extract and stir well.

2. Place the flour, baking powder, and baking soda in a bowl together with the milk and gradually add it little by little to the butter mixture. Add in the pistachios and beat everything for 2 minutes with the electric whisk until creamy.

3. Place the dough into a pastry bag with a round tip. Set walnut-sized balls of dough at a distance of 2 in apart on the baking sheet and bake whoopie pies for about 12 minutes in a hot oven until golden brown. Afterwards, allow 2 minutes on the baking sheet and then carefully transfer them to a cooling rack so that they can cool off completely.

A rose is a rose is a rose. No, making little butter cream roses is not as hard as it looks. I've got no years of experience, but only the right star tip for pastry bags. It really pays to invest in good tools, then it seems the roses bloom almost by themselves.

4. To make the butter cream, stir the butter and vanilla extract for at least 3 minutes until creamy. Sift powdered sugar and gradually add to the mix. Next add the rosewater and food coloring and beat for 3 minutes with the electric whisk. Place the butter cream into a pastry bag with a star tip or a plastic bag with the tip cut off. On the flat side of a whoopie pie half squirt a rose, on another half put a little butter cream and press the two halves together gently. Sprinkle with powdered sugar.

RASPBERRY CAKE TO GO

MAKES 4

Dough: 1 lemon   1/2 cup 1 tablespoon (125 g) butter (room temperature)   1/2 cup 2 tablespoon (125 g) sugar   2 eggs
1 1/2 cup 1 1/2 tablespoon (200 g) flour   1/2 packet baking powder   2 cup (250 g) raspberries (fresh or frozen)   butter for the glasses

Also: 4 oven-safe glasses with screw caps with a capacity around 1 cup (250 ml) ⇨ 140

These little cakes are really versatile: a beautiful dessert for barbecues, a nice gift for guests so that they still remember the next day what a lovely evening they had, a quick recipe for spontaneous visits and a sweet surprise for an outdoor picnic.

TIP
It's lovely if guests can take a taste directly from the juicy cake itself. Bind the glass with a rubber band or ribbon and stick a small, wooden fork (⇨ 140) in the cake.

1. Preheat the oven to 350 °F (180 °C) on the baking setting. Wash the lemon with hot water and wipe dry, finely grate the outer layer of the skin. Add butter to sugar and stir until creamy. Beat the eggs and add the lemon zest, then add the flour and the baking powder to the butter mixture and beat everything together.

2. Streak the glasses with butter and place a few raspberries in the bottom of the glasses. Alternate adding the batter with the raspberries in each glass so that they are filled to two-thirds. Use fresh-picked raspberries, or frozen raspberries that have been thawed. Finish with some raspberries on top. Place the glasses uncovered into the oven and bake for 25—30 minutes.

3. If you cover the glasses with a lid immediately after baking, the cake will stay preserved for at least 8 days in the refrigerator. To serve, preheat the oven to 215 °F (100 °C) on the baking setting, open the lids of the glasses and warm the cake for about 10 minutes.

The first encounter I had with Elettaria cardamom was when I tried a Swedish baking recipe a few years ago. I scrutinized these small, dried, green capsules with black seeds inside. This is supposed to taste good? Doesn't this spice belong in Arab cuisine, and even then doesn't it belong inside of a savory pot? The first bite refuted any doubts I had and Sultan Cardamom got a permanent spot in my tiny spice cabinet. He especially likes milk chocolate, Bundt cake, and liqueur. Since I can no longer refuse his request, there is now this fine combination in miniature.

TIP
The entire recipe becomes alcohol-free if you use orange juice instead of liqueur.

MINI BUNDT CAKES WITH ORANGE LIQUEUR

MAKES 24

Dough: 1/2 cup 1 1/2 tablespoon (70 g) powdered sugar   1/4 cup 1 tablespoon (70 g) butter (room temperature)   peel from 1/2 lemon   1 pinch salt   1/4 teaspoon ground cardamom   2 teaspoon orange liqueur (e.g. Cointreau)   1 egg   2 1/2 tablespoon (20 g) flour   2 teaspoon cocoa powder   1/4 cup 3 1/2 tablespoon (80 g) semolina   1/2 cup 1 1/2 tablespoon (80 g) milk chocolate couverture   butter and flour for the pan

Also: Mini Bundt cake mold for 24 (diameter: 1 2/3 in [4.3 cm], height: 1/2 in [1.5 cm]) ⟹ 141

1. Preheat oven to 400 °F (210 °C) on the baking setting. Grease the pan and sprinkle with flour. Stir the powdered sugar into a bowl with the butter and strain. Add and continue beating the lemon peel, salt, cardamom, orange liqueur, and egg into the butter mixture. Also sift the flour and cocoa powder into the bowl and add the semolina. Work everything into one homogenous mass with the electric whisk.

2. Chop the couverture into small pieces with a large knife and gently stir into the batter. Insert the dough into a pastry bag (or a plastic bag with the tip cut off) and squeeze into the mini Bundt cake pan — each indent should be filled to the brim.

3. Bake in the lower third of the oven for 11—12 minutes. Let cool on a wire rack for at least 30 minutes, then gently loosen from the mold.

MACARON LOLLIPOPS WITH BLUEBERRY BUTTER CREAM

MAKES 15–20

Hmm, who gives cake pops a run for their money? I tend to stick to small delicacies on lollipop sticks. This way they can be nibbled on more daintily. These macaron lollies with bows and tags can be eaten very neatly. They make me want to jump right into a red and white polka dot petticoat, put on some red lipstick, and spin around in circles with the macarons in sheer, sugary bliss. These treats are the truest essence of Mrs. K. Let's bake!

Dough: macaron dough ⇒ 16   1 pinch of red food coloring ⇒ 141

Cream: macaron cream ⇒ 16   1 tablespoon blueberry fruit powder ⇒ 140

Also: 15–20 lollipop sticks ⇒ 141

1. According to the basic recipe, bake red macarons and let them cool down. Make the butter cream follwing the recipe with blueberry fruit powder, put in the refrigerator for about 15 minutes, and then place into a pastry bag with a round tip or in a plastic bag with the corner cut off.

2. Now squirt a dab of butter cream on half of a macaron, insert a lollipop stick gently into the butter cream and cover with another half. Leave the lollies lying on a sheet of baking paper in a cool place overnight.

CAKE POP PRESENTS

MAKES 30–35

Dough: 1 chocolate cake ⇒ 15   cream ⇒ 12

Glaze: 2 1/2 cups (600 g) white cake icing (or white candy melts with 2—3 tablespoon vegetable fat shortening) ⇒ 140   7 tablespoon (100 g) gum paste ⇒ 116   7 tablespoon (100 g) fondant ⇒ 140   pinch of both green and pink food coloring ⇒ 141

Also: 1 skewer   Styrofoam block 12 in × 20 in × 4 in (30 cm × 50 cm × 10 cm)   35 lollipop sticks ⇒ 141   vegetable fat shortening for your hands, powdered sugar for the countertop

1. While the chocolate cake is baking, mix the ingredients for the cream. Form 30—35 cubes of cake and let sit cold about 15 minutes. Punch about 35 holes into the Styrofoam block with a skewer. Insert the lollipop sticks into the cubes, dip in the white icing (or candy melts) and place on the Styrofoam block until hardened completely intact.

2. Knead the gum paste with the fondant. For this, you should grease your hands with vegetable fat. Cut the mass into halves and color them both, either pink or green. On a countertop sprinkled with powdered sugar, shape each mass into a 1.5 mm thick roll and cut wide strips using a ruler to 4 mm. Cover this up with cling film for later use.

3. Create 30—35 fondant ribbons. To do so, bind the two ends of 2 in (5 cm) long strips so that they overlap 5 mm. Place another strip that is .7 in (2 cm) long in the center of the ribbons to form a loop and press firmly. To make the twisted ribbons, wrap the strips of fondant around a lollipop stick and allow to air dry. It is best to measure the length of the flattened bands prior to wrapping around the cake pops, so that they are not too short. Attach to the cake pops when the icing is still shining. Secure the bow with icing.

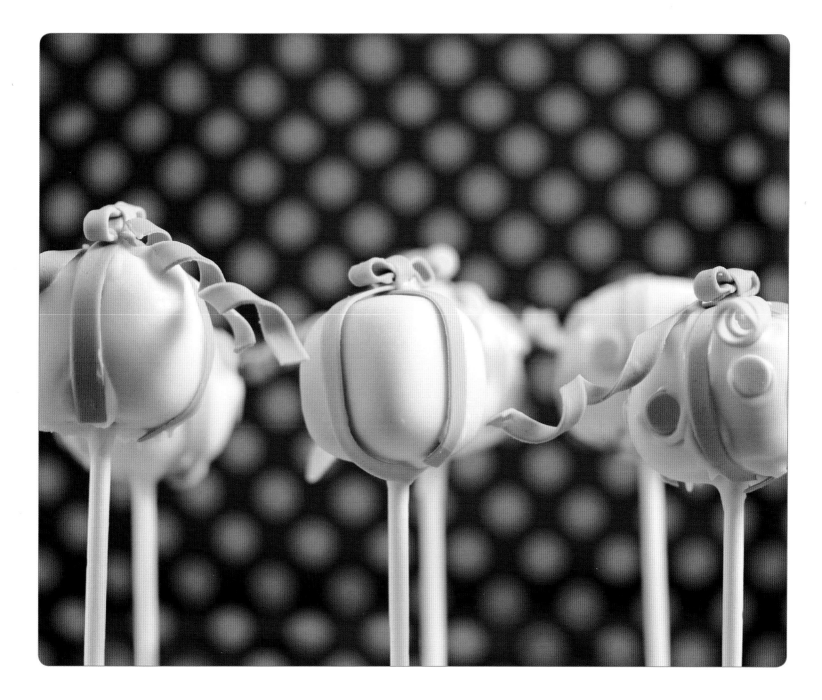

CARROT CAKE COOKIES WITH VANILLA CREAM

In conjunction with spices and a sensationally delicious cream cheese icing, this combination is a blast and even television tested. Mrs. K was just ever so crazy and participated in a baking show, and these cookies were served there among others.

TIP

Why not offer a cookie for dessert? Tie a strip of grease-proof paper and a ribbon around it and serve. Or give away as a gift. For that there is an especially good take away box (⟹ 141). With a jam jar label (⟹ 141) provided with a caption, you can get cookie creative.

MAKES 18–20

Dough: 6 tablespoon (85 g) butter (room temperature)   7 tablespoon (85 g) brown sugar   7 tablespoon (85 g) white sugar   1 egg
1/2 teaspoon vanilla extract ⟹ 141   1 cup 1/2 tablespoon (130 g) flour   1/2 teaspoon baking powder   1/2 teaspoon baking soda
1 pinch salt   1/2 teaspoon ground cinnamon   1 pinch ground nutmeg   1 small carrot   1 handful of macadamia nut kernels
1/2 cup 2 tablespoon (100 g) oat flakes

Cream: 7 tablespoon (100 g) cream cheese   3 1/2 tablespoon (50 g) butter (room temperature)   6 1/2 tablespoon (50 g) powdered sugar
1 teaspoon vanilla extract ⟹ 141

1. Preheat the oven to 320 °F (160 °C). Cover a tray with baking paper. Stir butter and both types of sugar until creamy. Add in egg and vanilla extract and mix well. Sieve flour and baking powder and mix with baking soda, salt, cinnamon and nutmeg. Add the flour mixture gradually to the butter mixture and work everything into a homogeneous mass.

2. Peel and finely grate the carrot. Chop the macadamia nuts coarsely with a large knife. Fold carrot, oat flakes, and nuts into the dough. With two teaspoons place hazelnut-sized pieces of dough on the baking sheet. Gently press the dough flat and bake in preheated oven for 13—15 minutes.

3. Meanwhile, for the filling mix cream cheese and butter together by stirring. Mix in powdered sugar and vanilla extract and let rest about 30 minutes. Once the cookies are cooled completely, squirt the cream onto one side of a cookie using a pastry bag and cover with another half. Lightly press together.

WINDMILL CUPCAKES

MAKES 12

....

Dough: vanilla cupcake batter ⟹ 78

Cream: vanilla cream ⟹ 78

Fondant: 2 cups 2 1/2 tablespoon (500 g) rolled fondant ⟹ 141   1 pinch each of pink, yellow, blue and green food
coloring ⟹ 141   sugar glue ⟹ 110

Also: 12-muffin tin   12 paper muffin holders   powdered sugar for the countertop   vegetable fat for your hands   rolling
pin ⟹ 141   circular cookie cutters (diameter about 2 1/2 in [6.5 cm])   smoother ⟹ 141

....

1. Prepare the cupcakes and butter cream (⟹ 78). Sprinkle the countertop with powdered sugar and grease hands with a little vegetable fat shortening. Softly knead the fondant until it has the desired elasticity. Pack 1 1/3 cup (300 g) fondant in a plastic bag and set it aside.

2. For the windmills split the remaining fondant 4/5 cup (200 g) into four equal parts and color each with either pink, yellow, blue or green food coloring (⟹ 124). This fondant will not be used immediately, once more put into a bag so it does not dry out. Spread the cupcakes with butter cream and cover with white fondant (⟹ 22).

3. Lay a square of paper 2 in × 2 in (4.5 cm × 4.5 cm) onto the thinly rolled, colored fondant and cut out the contour with a sharp knife. Cut the diagonals of the fondant quarters from the corners to about halfway. Carefully place each second peak to the center of the square and lightly press. Form a small ball out of some fondant (preferably in a different color), moisten with a little sugar glue and place on the center. Brush the bottom sides of the windmill with sugar glue and attach it to the cupcake.

Only once in a while do you get to be a fly on the wall in some of the best bakeries. When you do it's a wonderful chance to watch, learn, and write down the best recipes. Test them out and be amazed. A little bit of new knowledge can lead to some fun creations.
I continue baking diligently — with love. How else could it be with delicious windmill cupcakes in the most delicate colors?

CRINKLE COOKIES

MAKES AROUND 40

....

Dough: 1 3/4 cup (225 g) plain couverture chocolate   1 cup (200 g) brown sugar   4 tablespoon (63 ml) macadamia nut oil (or sunflower oil)   2 eggs   1 teaspoon vanilla extract ⟹ 141   1 cup (135 g) flour   1 teaspoon baking powder   1 pinch of salt   1/2 cup 3 tablespoon (75 g) walnuts   7/8 cup (100 g) powdered sugar

....

1. Melt the couverture in a water bath, let cool down again and mix with sugar and oil. Add the eggs and stir until creamy with an electric whisk. Add vanilla extract, flour, baking powder and salt and work everything into a homogeneous mass. Chop the walnuts with a large knife and mix in. Cover the dough with plastic wrap and let rest for about 2 hours.

2. Preheat the oven to 356 °F (180 °C) on the baking setting. Cover a baking tray with parchment paper. Shape the dough into balls with a diameter of about 1 in (2.5 cm.) Sieve the powdered sugar into a small bowl, roll the balls in it and place them at a distance of 2 in (5—6 cm) from each other on the baking sheet. Bake the cookies in a hot oven for 12—14 minutes.

3. If you would like to serve the cookie perched on a glass of milk with a straw through the middle, then bring out a cookie cutter and prick a hole in the center of the cookie when it is still warm.

The best thing about these cookies is that you don't need any pastry bags, cookie cutters, or colored sprinkles. The giant crispy cookies are therefore entirely without decoration and still look great. Add a glass of milk and the day is saved.

TIP
Cut or punch a heart, circle or a design of your choice out of a small paper bag. Fill a plastic bag with cookies, seal well, and place it in the paper bag. Decorate the bag with colored paper and a gift tag and you have a little something.

DIRNDL COOKIE POPS

MAKES AROUND 12

....

Dough: Favorite sugar cookie dough ⇒ 18

Glaze: 1 1/3 cup (300 g) fondant ⇒ 140   1/2 teaspoon of both red and pink food coloring ⇒ 141   Sugar glue ⇒ 116
Or 2/3 cup (80 g) powdered sugar

Also: Circular cookie cutters 2.5 in and 3 in (diameter 6.5 cm and 8 cm)   12 oven safe lollipop sticks   Some vegetable fat for your hands   Powdered sugar for the countertop   Rolling pin ⇒ 141   Ridged cookie cutter, diameter 3 in (7.5 cm)   Heart cookie cutters 2 in × 1 in (4.5 cm × 3 cm)

....

⇒ 18 ⇒ 140 ⇒ 141 ⇒ 116 ⇒ 141 ⇒ 19

1. Prepare the dough and roll out to a 6 mm thickness. Cut out twelve round cookies with diameters of 3 in (8 cm) attach oven safe lollipop sticks (⇒ 19) and bake. Place the cookies on a sheet of baking paper for decorating.

2. Grease hands with some vegetable fat shortening and knead the fondant until soft. Color about 1/2 cup (120 g) fondant with pink food coloring and 1/2 teaspoon (60 g) with red food coloring. The rest of the fondant remains white.

3. Successively roll out the pink, white and red fondant to a thickness of about 1 mm onto a countertop sprinkled with powdered sugar. Cut out six pink and six white wavy circles of 3 in (7.5 cm) in diameter with the ridged cookie cutter and six pink and six white circles of 2.5 in (6 cm) in diameter. Cut out twelve hearts from the red fondant.

4. Coat the bottom side of the wavy circles (pink or white) with sugar glue and stick on the cookie. Then apply a normal circle of fondant and finally a heart. Instead of sugar glue you can mix 1/3 cup 1 teaspoon (80 g) powdered sugar with a few drops of water to a paste.

Hmm!

The beauty in these cookies is
that you don't need a steady
hand. Here you simply take away
what is cut out with the tool
and the result is a cookie that
looks like it was made by a pro-
fessional. The colors and their
cutters could of course vary
according to your mood.

TIP
In a striped paper bag(⇨ 141)
cut or punch a circle and line
with a cellophane bag. Throw in
the lollipop and seal with a
ribbon.

For a moment you must have thought: "Wait, there's also frozen foods in here?" Hehe, no, I tricked you, it's still a baking book. But because I like ice cream so much, and it definitely counts as one of the itty bitty things that makes you happy, I cheated and found a way to worm it into this book. An ode to ice cream in the form of an optical illusion or "the ice cream coup."

There are two ways to make cupcakes in a waffle cone. The simplest is to bake the cupcake in the waffle cone. But the cone could break or deform during the baking process — unless you can find soft waffle cones without a tip. The elegant, but slightly more expensive option is to bake the cupcakes and then to maneuver them into the waffle cone. I prefer option two. They both taste like a chocolate-y revelation, no question.

ICE CREAM CUPCAKES

MAKES 24 MINI CUPCAKES OR 12 CUPCAKES IN CONES

....

Dough: 1/3 cup (75 g) butter   1/2 teaspoon vanilla extract ⇨ 141   2 cup (250 g) flour   1/2 cup 1 tablespoon (50 g) cocoa powder
1 teaspoon baking powder   1 teaspoon baking soda   1 cup 1 1/2 tablespoon (220 g) sugar   1 cup 1 tablespoon (250 ml) milk   1 egg

Cream: 1 1/2 cup (200 g) dark couverture chocolate   1 1/3 cup (200 g) powdered sugar   1/2 cup 1 tablespoon (50 g) cocoa powder
1 1/3 cup (300 g) butter (room temperature)   ½ teaspoon vanilla extract ⇨ 141

For decoration: 3/4 cup 2 tablespoon (200 g) dark cake frosting   1/3 cup 1 tablespoon (50 g) grated chocolate

Also: mini cupcake tin for 24 cupcakes   24 mini paper cupcake holders   12—15 ice cream waffle cones ⇨ 140

....

1. Preheat the oven to 347 °F (175 °C) on the baking setting. Stick the paper cupcake holders into the cupcake tin. Put butter and vanilla extract in a small saucepan, melt at a low temperature and set aside to cool down. Strain flour, cocoa powder and baking powder into a large bowl. Add baking soda and sugar. Whisk together milk and egg in a small bowl. Gradually add the butter and milk mixture to the dry ingredients and stir well. Fill the paper cupcake holders two-thirds full with the batter and bake for 15—17 minutes in the oven. Conduct the toothpick test!

2. For the buttercream melt the couverture in a water bath and set aside to cool down. Sieve powdered sugar and cocoa powder. Beat the butter at least 7 minutes until creamy. Gradually stir in the powdered sugar and cocoa until a smooth, clump-free cream forms. Add the chocolate and vanilla extract and beat for at least 5 minutes with the electric whisk or KitchenAid.

3. The butter cream can be worked with immediately. Place it into a pastry bag with a pointed tip. Remove the cupcakes from the paper holders. Inject a little of the butter cream into the top of the ice cream cone and put two cupcakes in the waffle cone. Sometimes you have to split the cupcake bottom in two halves in order to be able to better push it into the waffle cone. Between the two cupcakes also inject a small amount of butter cream, so that the top has a better grip. Now squeeze out the crown of butter cream on top of the top cupcake and let cool for 10 minutes.

4. While the cupcakes are in the refrigerator, warm the cake icing and leave to cool down again. Spread the glaze onto the cupcakes using a small spoon and sprinkle the grated chocolate on top.

I SCREAM,
YOU SCREAM,
WE ALL SCREAM
FOR ICE CREAM!

MACARONS WITH STAMPS

Aren't we all a little Alice in Wonderland? Suppose I take a bite now, will I grow from teeny tiny into a giant? If a hopping white rabbit comes around the corner and the Cheshire Cat appears out of nowhere, then I couldn't believe myself anymore. But it is too tempting ... close your eyes and go!

MAKES 15–20

Dough: Macaron dough ⇒ 16   1 pinch pink food coloring

Cream: Butter cream ⇒ 16

Also: Black food coloring ⇒ 141   Letter template ⇒ 141

1. According to the basic recipe from page 16, bake pink macarons. Stamp half of the macaron halves. To do so, use the templates to paint letters on the macarons with the black food coloring and press down very carefully on the surface. Lay the stamped halves on a sheet of baking paper to dry.

2. In the meantime make the cream, place in the refrigerator for about 15 minutes. Now squirt a dab of butter cream onto half of a macaron and cover with another half.

LUCKY COOKIES

MAKES AROUND 12 LARGE AND 12 SMALL COOKIES

. . . .

Dough: 1/2 quantity of favorite sugar cookie dough ⟹ 18

Glaze: 1/2 amount of egg white spray glaze or meringue powder glaze ⟹ 21   1 pinch of pink food coloring ⟹ 141

Also: 2 mushroom cookie cutters 2.5 in × 2 in and 2 in × 1 in (6 cm × 5 cm and 4.5 cm × 3.5 cm)   Pastry bag with round tip

. . . .

The ultimate bearers of good fortune present themselves this time as a cookie. They have made themselves totally pretty and work well for driver's license tests, job interviews, and very important moments that bring new beginnings. Naturally, you simply give away luck with these. Who could say no?

1. Follow the basic recipe from page 18 to prepare the sugar cookie dough. After you roll out the dough, cut from it twelve large and twelve small mushroom shaped cookies. Then bake. Let cool down and put the glaze on a piece of baking paper.

2. Prepare half the amount of egg white spray glaze or glaze of meringue powder and distribute equally into two bowls. Color the contents of one bowl pink. Add a few drops of water until you get the desired consistency for applying the rim of sugar.

3. Place a small amount of glaze into a pastry bag with a round tip and squeeze out a rim of icing in pink and white on the cookie. Put aside the pastry bag with the white glaze.

4. Thin out the rest of the pink glaze in both bowls with a few drops of water to fill out the cookies and spread onto the cookies (⟹ 20/21). Once the surface is somewhat dried, dab spots on the mushroom with white icing in a pastry bag. Let cookies dry overnight on the baking paper.

TIP

Here I have used a glassine baggy
(⇨141), which normally is used
for storage of postage stamps. Put
in the lucky cookies and sew the
bag closed with a needle, thread
and a few stitches — even begin-
ners like me can manage it. Stamp
on a solid colored paper the word
"luck" with an alphabet stamp set,
cut a small piece of ribbon, and
clip on a small clothes pin to the
bag. The tiny package of luck is
ready.

COOKIES WITH STAMPS

MAKES 15–30 COOKIES

....

Dough: Favorite sugar cookie dough ⇨ 18

Also: 2–3 oven safe lollipop sticks ⇨ 141   Cookie cutters, stamp set ⇨ 141   Ribbons

....

1. According to the basic recipe from page 18 prepare the dough and roll out to 1/4 in (6 mm) thick. Preheat the oven to 400 °F (200 °C) on the baking setting. Cut out cookies with the desired cookie cutter shapes, place on the baking sheet and stamp on the cookies carefully.

2. Cut lollipop sticks to about 1 inch (2.5 cm) long. Stick them in the dough (and bake), later the ribbon will be affixed to these.

3. Bake the cookies in the oven for 7–8 minutes. Caution! The cookies should not brown. Leave cookies on a wire rack to cool down and remove the lollipop sticks. Then secure a small ribbon to the cookie through the hole and then they can be given away.

Is paper's sole prerogative to be stamped? No, not anymore! That time is long gone. Today everything can be stamped! My favorites in the stamp universe? Stamped cookies! They are quickly baked and beautified in no time as a loving gift or a souvenir. A little thing that makes giving even nicer.

SWEETS TO MAKE

YOU HAPPY

CHEESCAKE #1 WITH PEANUTS OR STRAWBERRY TOPPING

MAKES 1 CAKE AT 10 IN (26 CM) OR 2 CAKES AT 7 IN (18 CM)

....

Crust: 1 1/3 cup (150 g) wholemeal shortbread cookies   1/4 cup (60 g) butter   2 tablespoons sugar   1 pinch ground cinnamon   butter for the mold

Cheesecake: 3 cups 7 tablespoon (800 g) cream cheese (room temperature)   3/4 cup 2 tablespoon (200 g) sour cream (room temperature)   1 cup (200 g) sugar   2 teaspoon vanilla extract ⟹ 141   4 eggs   3 tablespoon (25 g) corn starch   1/4 cup (50 ml) milk

Easy-Peasy Snickers topping: 3—4 peanut candy bars ⟹ 106   1/2 cup (150 g) caramel spread ⟹ 62

Strawberry topping: 7 cup (1 kg) strawberries   2 tablespoons sugar   1 teaspoon lemon juice

Also: 1 springform pan 10 in (26 cm) or 2 springform pans 7 in (18 cm)

....

1. Preheat the oven to 360 °F (180 °C) on the baking setting. Grease the springform pan (s) thoroughly with butter and wrap with three layers of aluminum foil from bottom to top, sealing them so that later no water can enter into the mold in the water bath.

2. Crush the cookies in a food chopper or simply place them in a plastic bag and smash with a rolling pin until they are crushed. Melt the butter in a small saucepan and let cool down again. Mix cookie crumbs, liquid butter, sugar and cinnamon and press down on the bottom of the mold (s). Smooth it with your fingers or a large spoon. Place the mold (s) in the refrigerator for about 30 minutes.

If there was a poll for the #1 cheesecake, I would give my vote in support of this superb version. The method of baking in a water bath and the use of cream cheese instead of cottage cheese ensures an on-the-tongue-melt-down and a tiptop look. Ohhs and mmmmhhhs guaranteed!

Whoever wants to turn their cheesecake into a deluxe version must only decide between two toppings.

TIP
Who says that cheesecake cannot work as a wedding cake? With a chic banner, neatly hand painted, it is even quite appropriate for the most beautiful day of your life.

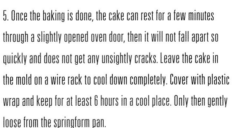

3. To make the cheesecake stir the cream cheese and sour cream with sugar and vanilla extract until smooth. Mix the eggs separately. Lastly, incorporate the corn starch and milk carefully. The whole thing is now relatively liquid and exactly how it should be. Carefully pour the filling onto the cake base and smooth.

4. Now comes the part that makes the cake so airy - the water bath! For this, fill the drip pan of the oven with hot water - it should be about 1 in (2.5 cm) high. Place in the springform pan(s) with the tinfoil on top and bake for about 60 minutes until the cake is uniformly high, and the surface is a bit golden brown.

5. Once the baking is done, the cake can rest for a few minutes through a slightly opened oven door, then it will not fall apart so quickly and does not get any unsightly cracks. Leave the cake in the mold on a wire rack to cool down completely. Cover with plastic wrap and keep for at least 6 hours in a cool place. Only then gently loose from the springform pan.

6. For the peanut topping break the chocolate bars into small pieces and place on the cake. Spread a small spoonful of caramel cream onto the cake.

For the strawberry topping wash the strawberries, pat dry and remove stems. Purée half of the berries, pass through a fine sieve and season to taste with sugar and 1 teaspoon lemon juice. Cut the rest of the strawberries into quarters and place on the cake. Drizzle on the strawberry purée just before serving the cake.

CHOCOLATE WHOOPIE PIES

MAKES 10

. . . .

A piece of fashion amongst baked goods? Oh! Since at least the 1920s, these sweet sandwiches have conquered the American heart and also mine. Do you expect crispy cookies at the sight of them? Far from it. These are two loose, soft cake halves with a cream filling. Whoopie Pies require an eating stance similar to a burger as it's risky to eat them with one hand.

Whoever enjoys these sweet sandwiches and wishes to bake them professionally can also purchase a special whoopie pie mold (⇨ 141). With these the halves turn out the same size, but the baking time is several minutes longer.

Dough: 1 egg   3/4 cup (150 g) sugar   1/3 cup (75 g) butter   2 tablespoon (25 ml) milk   1/2 cup (125 g) vanilla yogurt   1/2 teaspoon vanilla extract ⇨ 140   3/4 cup 3 tablespoon (80 g) cocoa powder   1 1/2 cup 1 1/2 tablespoon (200 g) flour   3/4 teaspoon baking soda 1/4 teaspoon baking powder

Cream: 2 1/3 cup 2 tablespoon (80 g) powdered sugar   3/4 cup (170 g) butter (room temperature)   1 jar (1 1/2 cup or 213 g) Vanilla Marshmallow Fluff ⇨ 140

. . . .

1. Add egg and sugar to a bowl and vigorously beat until the mixture is light and creamy. Melt the butter in a small saucepan on the stove and set aside to cool down. Whisk the yogurt, milk and vanilla extract in a container and add to the sugar mixture. Add the butter and process everything with an electric whisk to a homogeneous mass.

2. Sieve cocoa powder, flour, baking soda and baking powder and gradually add to the creamy mixture and stir well. Place the dough in the refrigerator for about 20 minutes. Meanwhile, preheat the oven to 340 °F (170 °C) and line two baking sheets with parchment paper.

3. Spread 2 cooled tablespoons of the dough in heaps of 1.5 in (at a distance of 1—1.5 in [3—4 cm]) on the baking paper. Each sheet should have no more than 10 pieces. Once both trays are filled, push them in the oven for about 12—13 minutes. Conduct the toothpick test! The whoopie pie halves can cool down on a wire rack.

4. For the cream, mix the powdered sugar with the butter until creamy. Gradually add Marshmallow Fluff. Beat for 3 minutes with the electric whisk and then put in the refrigerator for about 30 minutes. Now fill the whoopie pies with cream and put them together. For an easier application of the cream filling, use a pastry bag or a small plastic bag with the tip cut off. Of course, it also works with two teaspoons. Whoopie pies hold up well for about 2—3 days.

TIP

Whoopie Pies can also make great gifts — distributed preferably on baking day. For this purpose there are perfectly designed smoothie cups (⇨ 141), which can be beautified quickly with a great gift tag and a few cute ribbons.

BLACK & WHITE CAKE POPS

MAKES 30-35

Dough: 1 chocolate or vanilla cake ⟹ 15   cream ⟹ 12

Glaze: 2 1/2 cup 1 tablespoon (600 g) white or dark cake frosting, ⟹ 70   Striped wafer sticks (and 1/2 cup (100 g) white or dark cake frosting)

Also: 1 skewer   Styrofoam block 12 in × 20 in × 4 in (30 cm × 50 cm × 10 cm) ⟹ 141   30—35 lollipop sticks ⟹ 141

1. According to the basic recipe from page 15 bake a chocolate or vanilla cake and mix with the ingredients for the cream. Form 30—35 cake balls and let them rest about 15 minutes. Since the cake pops are put to dry in the styrofoam block, drill about 35 holes in the Styrofoam block with the skewer. Then attach the lollipop sticks to the cake balls according to the recipe and glaze with white or dark cake frosting. To dry, plug the lollies into the Styrofoam block.

2. If have you chosen the wafer sticks as the main decoration, it is best to attach them to the cake pops when the glaze still shines a little. If you prefer to decorate the cake pops with some chocolate icing, then melt the glaze in a small, glass bowl in a water bath or in the microwave. Place the warm icing into a small plastic bag, cut off a corner of it and craftily glaze the cake pops with it. To dry, plug the lollies into the Styrofoam block.

PINK VELVET CAKE

MAKES 1 CAKE, 12 SLICES

Dough: 7 egg whites   1 egg   1 1/2 cups (360 ml) whole milk (room temperature)   1 tablespoon vanilla extract ⟹ 141   1/2 bottle almond extract   3 2/3 cup (460 g) flour   2 1/4 cup (450 g) sugar   1 packet baking powder   1 teaspoon salt   3/4 cup (170 g) butter (room temperature)   1/3 cup 1 tablespoon (85 g) vegetable fat (e.g. Palmin soft)   1 teaspoon pink food coloring ⟹ 141   Butter for the mold

Cream: 2 1/2 cup (575 g) butter (room temperature)   1 pinch of pink food coloring ⟹ 141   5 cup (600 g) powdered sugar   1/3 cup (70 ml) milk   1 teaspoon vanilla extract ⟹ 141

Also: 2 springform pans (diameter 8 in [20 cm])   Pie underlayer made of cardboard (diameter 8 in [20 cm]) or cakeboard ⟹ 140   Lazy Susan ⟹ 140

1. Preheat the oven to 356 °F (180 °C) on the baking setting. Grease the springform pan. Whisk together the egg whites and whole eggs, 1/2 cup (120 ml) milk, vanilla extract and almond extract in a medium sized bowl and set aside. Sift the flour and mix with sugar, baking powder and salt in a large bowl. Add butter, vegetable shortening and remaining milk alternately and mix with the electric whisk or KitchenAid. Gradually add the egg mixture and beat everything until creamy.

2. Distribute the dough into four bowls (these are each about 2 cup [415 g]) and color in four different shades of pink. Pour the contents of two bowls into two springform pans. Smooth the surface. Bake the cake on the middle rack in the hot oven for about 24 minutes. Don't forget the toothpick test. Let the finished cake cool down on a wire rack for 10 minutes, loosen from the mold and let cool completely. Wash the molds, grease, and bake two more crusts from the remaining dough.

3. For the cream, whisk the butter for at least 7 minutes until creamy. Gradually add the powdered sugar. Add milk, vanilla extract and pink food coloring. Beat for another 5 minutes. The butter cream can continue to be worked with immediately.

"Oh, there's marzipan in it!" The most enthusiastic comments about this cake are usually given within the first five seconds after the person has had their first bite.

I quite look forward to the resonance and the facial expressions, sometimes while holding my breath. A more honest criticism is normally given only by persons under age six.

Yes, this heavenly little cake truly tastes of marzipan and the quick-to-dissolve pink butter. cream perfectly completes its amazing taste.

4. Now assemble the cake: Cut the upper crust and the unevenness of each cake off with a sharp knife (serrated). Measure and cut the cake underlayer (8 in [20 cm]). This allows a better transport of the cake to the cake plate later on. Spread a very thin layer of buttercream on the middle of a rotary plate, so that the cake does not slip. Place the pie crust on the turntable.

5. Place the first dough base with the cross section viewable on top of the cake crust and distribute a 1/2 in (1.5 cm) thick layer of butter cream on the entire surface with a palette or a large knife. It is perfectly okay if the butter cream is oozing out on the sides, which can be corrected later. Proceed likewise with the second and third layers. The fourth layer is placed on the cake with the cross section face down. Should the cake still have some irregularities straighten them out with a sharp knife.

6. Spread a fine layer of butter cream evenly over the cake. Slowly rotate the turntable with one hand and hold the other perpendicular to the side of the cake. This quickly results in a uniformly thick layer. Leave the cake in the refrigerator for 30 minutes, then spread with a second layer of butter cream. If the dough still peeks through in some places, repeat this process again. Let the cake rest again and remove from the refrigerator 30 minutes before serving.

CARAMEL MACARONS

MAKES 15-20

....

Creme caramel (dulce de leche): 1 can sweetened condensed milk ⟹ 141

Dough: macaron dough ⟹ 16   1/2 teaspoon cocoa

....

1. Remove the label from the condensed milk. Fill a large pot three-quarters full with water. Bring the water to a boil and cover with a lid. The can should be covered during the cooking process that follows with water.

2. The milk now needs to cook for 2—3 hours until it thickens, gets a brownish coloration and a caramel flavor. To accelerate the process a pressure cooker can be used, then it takes a whole 20 minutes.

3. According to the basic recipe from page 16 bake yellow macarons. Instead of food coloring the cocoa colors the macarons to a wonderful caramel shade. Simply mix the egg whites with the almond mixture. Let the crème caramel (dulce de leche) cool down, spread on half of the macaron halves and cover with the rest.

Macarons and caramel in combination? This must be heaven. Crispy macarons with a melted caramel cream just make everyone happy and also look quite charming.

Here I made the dulce de leche itself. This caramel cream is a native of South America that tastes rather exquisite.

TIP
If you don't want to wait until the dulce de leche is ready after baking the macarons, you can also fall back on pre-made caramel cream (eg, of Bonne Maman) or dulce de leche in a jar.

WHOOPIE PIES WITH WHITE CHOCOLATE AND RASPBERRIES

MAKES 16

I have to admit it, I'm pretty in love with these whoopie pies. They combine the juiciness of a cake, the elegance of macaroons and the pretty little tops of cupcakes. For too long they have been hiding from me. When I discovered them the first time and then saw all the other ways of channeling my passion for cooking into the mixing bowl, I was more than obsessed.

Here is a definite favorite in my small pie universe. The raspberry whoopie pies with white chocolate. Yum!

Dough: 1/2 cup 1 teaspoon (125 g) butter (room temperature)   3/4 cup 1 tablespoon (165 g) sugar   1 egg   1 teaspoon vanilla extract ⇒ 141
2 1/3 cup 1 tablespoon (300 g) flour   1 1/2 teaspoon baking powder   1/2 teaspoon baking soda   1/2 cup 2 tablespoon (150 ml) milk
1 cup 2 tablespoon (150 g) white chocolate

cream: 5 egg whites   3/4 cup 2 tablespoon (175 g) sugar   3/4 cup 2 tablespoon (200 g) butter (room temperature)   3 1/4 cup (400 g)
raspberries

1. Preheat the oven to 360 °F (180 °C) on the baking setting and cover two baking sheets with parchment paper. Beat butter and sugar in a bowl until creamy. Add egg and vanilla extract. Sieve flour, baking powder and baking soda and add gradually to the butter mixture. Also stir in the milk. Chop the chocolate with a large knife into fine pieces and gently stir into the mixture.

2. Using two teaspoons, distribute heaps of dough at a distance of about 2 in (5 cm) on the baking paper. Bake the cake until golden brown for about 10—15 minutes. Then, let rest 2 minutes on the baking paper and then cool completely on a wire rack.

3. For the butter cream, beat the egg whites and sugar in a glass bowl in a water bath with a whisk until frothy. The bowl should not touch the hot water so that the egg does not curdle. Keep stirring until the sugar has completely drained. Remove the bowl from the water bath. With an electric whisk or a KitchenAid, beat the egg white mixture about 10 minutes, until firm, white, and cold.

4. Add the softened butter in small pieces. The mass may look slightly curdled, but that is ok. After a few minutes, a smooth cream forms. Purée 1 cup (150 g) raspberries with a hand blender, pass through a fine sieve and mix the collected purée into the butter cream.

5. Place the butter cream into a pastry bag or a plastic bag with the tip cut off and spray on the flat side of a whoopie pie half. Decorate with some raspberries, apply a little butter cream onto a second half and gently press the two halves together.

SWEET & SALTY CAKE POPS

MAKES 30-35

....

Dough: 1 chocolate cake ⇨ 15 cream ⇨ 12

Icing: 3 cup (600 g) peanut butter Candy Melts ⇨ 140   2—3 tablespoons vegetable fat   1 1/3 cup (300 g) whole milk cake icing
2/3 cup (100 g) toasted, salted peanuts

Also: 1 skewer   Styrofoam block 12 in × 20 in × 4 in (30 cm × 50 cm × 10 cm)   35 lollipop sticks ⇨ 141

....

Salty little nuts in milk chocolate? This makes my stomach do flips and my taste buds celebrate with joy. Sweet and salty — this duet caused true happiness.
Do you want to design your own cup? Then grab a porcelain pen and fire away! If you mess up, it's not so bad. The ink can be removed easily with nail polish remover.

1. According to the basic recipe from page 15, bake a chocolate cake and mix the ingredients for the icing. Form 30—35 cake balls and let them sit about 15 minutes. Since the cake pops will be placed to dry in a Styrofoam block, drill about 35 holes in the Styrofoam block now with a skewer. Then attach the lollipop sticks to the cake balls following the recipe. Glaze with peanut butter Candy Melts completely and allow to dry completely intact in the styrofoam block.

2. Also melt the cake icing, turn over the cake pops so that they are facing head down to half dip into the icing and allow to drizzle. Chop the peanuts coarsely and sprinkle on the icing while it is still glistening.

TIP

Here I have mini-cupcake paper used as a cuff. Simply pierce a small hole in the bottom of the cupcake wrappers and insert the lollipop stick. For the pendant I have punched and stamped a piece of cardboard with a wave punch. So prick two small holes and gently pull over the stick.

BLUEBERRY CUPCAKES WITH VANILLA CREAM

MAKES 12

Dough: 1 1/3 cup 1 1/2 tablespoon (180 g) flour   1/2 tablespoon baking powder   1 pinch of salt   1/2 cup (110 g) butter (room temperature)
3/4 cup 2 teaspoon (175 g) sugar   2 eggs   1 teaspoon vanilla extract ⟹ 141   2/3 cup (155 ml) milk   1/2 cup (75 g) blueberries (fresh or frozen)

Cream: 3/4 cup (175 ml) milk   5 teaspoon flour   1 2/3 cup (200 g) powdered sugar   3/4 cup 2 tablespoon (200 g) butter (room temperature)
1 packet vanilla sugar

Also: 12-muffin tin   12 paper cupcake holders pastry bag with star tip ⟹ 141

NO. I have unfortunately no photos for you of this small blueberry treat! They disappeared so quickly, really no one could press the shutter release in time. No wonder! Blueberries with fluffy vanilla butter cream? I actually thought to myself ... Who can resist that? "I need the recipe!" my dear neighbor exclaimed. Sure, you can have it!

1. Preheat the oven to 350 °F (175 °C) on the baking setting. Cover the muffin tin with cupcake holders. Mix flour, baking powder and salt. Stir butter and sugar until creamy. Add the eggs one after the other; stir in the vanilla extract. Gradually add the flour mixture and the milk. Gently stir in the blueberries with a spoon. Caution! Leave a few left over for decorating. Fill the cupcake holders three-quarters with batter and bake for about 25 minutes. Don't forget the toothpick test.

2. For the vanilla butter cream heat milk and flour in a saucepan while stirring until a pudding-like mass forms. Stir again in the cold water bath. To do this simply fill the sink with cold water and put in the pot.

3. Sieve the powdered sugar. Thoroughly stir butter, baking powder and vanilla sugar in a bowl. Now gradually stir in the flour mixture until a homogeneous mass is formed and the sugar has completely dissolved. Place in the refrigerator for about 10 minutes.

4. Inject the cooled cupcakes with the butter cream using a pastry bag with a star tip 1 tablespoon (14 mm). Then throw on a few blueberries elegantly with a flip of the wrist. Anyone who wants can beautify the cake additionally with a cupcake topper (⇨ 140) or a lollipop stick.

BROWNIES WITH PINE NUTS AND PISTACHIOS

MAKES 9

Dough: 1 3/4 cup 1 tablespoon (240 g) bitter dark chocolate   3/4 cup 2 teaspoon (180 g) butter   4 eggs   1 1/2 cup (300 g) sugar   1 3/4 cup 2 tablespoon (180 g) flour   1/3 bottle rum flavoring   1/3 cup (50 g) pine nuts   1/3 cup 1 tablespoon (50 g) pistachios   3/4 cup 1 tablespoon (200 g) of whole milk   Butter for the mold

Also: 1 baking pan 9 in × 9 in (23 cm × 23 cm)

1. Preheat the oven to 360 °F (180 °C) on the baking setting. Grease the baking pan and sprinkle with flour. Melt chocolate and butter in a water bath and let cool down again. Successively add in eggs, sugar, rum flavoring, flour and nuts and mix well.

2. Fill the dough into the mold and bake for about 30 minutes in the oven. Conduct the toothpick test. Let the cake stand for 10 minutes in the mold and gently place on a wire rack to cool down.

3. According to package directions, warm and spread the icing on the brownies. To serve, cut the brownies into nine pieces.

You can bake these super juicy, chocolatey brownies in a jiffy, and they will be eaten just as quickly. If you serve the brownies as a whole, you can still print a powdered sugar pattern.

TITEL   Brownies

AUS DER KÜCHE VON... Deni

REZEPT

TIP

This chocolate bomb with a ribbon à la Martha Stewart is perfectly bakery-appropriate. To do this you place a paper template over the glazed, dried brownie before dusting with powdeed sugar. Depending on the season and occasion there are of course also star stencils for Christmas, a number template for a birthday, or a template heart for Valentine's Day.

BANANA CARAMEL CUPCAKES
MAKES 12

....

Dough: 3 cup (300 g) flour   2 teaspoon baking powder   1 teaspoon baking soda   1/2 cup (100 g) sugar
1/2 cup (100 g) white chocolate   1 1/4 cup (300 ml) milk   3 ripe bananas   1/3 cup (70 ml) sunflower oil

Cream: 3 egg whites   1/2 cup 1 tablespoon (120 g) sugar   1/2 cup 1 1/2 tablespoon (135 g) butter (room temperature)
3—4 tablespoons caramel spread ⇨ 62 or ⇨ 141

Also: 12-muffin tin   12 paper cupcake holders

....

1. Preheat the oven to 350 °F (175 °C) on the baking setting. Place cupcake holders in the muffin tin. Sieve flour and baking powder in a bowl. Add baking soda and sugar and mix well. Chop the white chocolate into small pieces with a large knife and add to the flour mixture.

2. Stir in milk and sunflower oil with the hand mixer. Purée the bananas and stir into the batter. Fill up the cupcake holders halfway and bake for 20—25 minutes. Toothpick test! Remove the cupcakes from the paper holders and let cool down on a wire rack.

3. For the butter cream heat the egg whites with the sugar in a glass bowl in a water bath with a whisk to about 150 °F (65 °C) (not hot!). Make sure that the bowl does not touch the water in the pot, otherwise the egg whites could coagulate. Once the sugar has completely dissolved, take the glass bowl from the water bath and beat the mixture for at least 10 minutes until stiff and cold with the electric whisk or KitchenAid.

Shall I tell you something? My first butter cream I made this way completely failed. I can not even say what happened in hindsight. I observed and read through the recipe precisely. Sometimes there's simply a worm in it: it's Monday, it's a full moon and you got up on the wrong side of the bed. All at the same time. It's all worth it when the second trial runs so smoothly, without constantly looking at the recipe, that it feels like it's running by itself. Had I immediately thrown in the towel, I never would have enjoyed these banana cupcakes with dulce de leche butter cream. What luck there was a second attempt.

4. Cut the butter into small cubes and add gradually while stirring. Sometimes the the mass looks a bit curdled, but just be patient, after a few minutes, everything goes back to a smooth cream. (If this is not the case, then you can warm the cream again for a few seconds in the water bath.) Add the caramel spread and stir again vigorously. Fill a pastry bag with a star tip with the butter cream and decorate the cooled cupcakes. If you like, spoon a little more caramel on top.

TIP
In a small smoothie cup ( 141), the whole thing becomes a cupcake to go.

MINI CINNAMON ROLLS

MAKES 25-30

Dough: 2 1/2 tablespoon (40 g) butter   1/2 cup (125 ml) milk   1 tablespoon (15 g) fresh yeast   3 tablespoon (40 g) sugar   1/4 teaspoon salt   1/4 teaspoon ground cardamom   1 2/3 cup (270 g) flour   flour for the countertop

Stuffing: 1/4 cup 1 tablespoon (75 g) butter (room temperature)   1/4 cup 2 tablespoon (100 g) sugar   1 tablespoon cinnamon   1 egg   1 teaspoon milk

1. Cover a baking sheet with parchment paper. For the dough, melt the butter in a small saucepan. Add the milk, warming slightly (about 100 °F [38 °C]) and remove from heat. Add and stir yeast, sugar, salt and cardamom and cook until all ingredients are completely dissolved.

2. Put the flour into a large bowl and add the liquid ingredients. With a spatula mix the ingredients. Lastly, knead the dough with your hands thoroughly. If it sticks to your fingers, add some flour. Shape the dough into a ball and cover with a kitchen towel for about 30 minutes in a warm place to rest.

3. Dust the countertop with flour. Knead the dough again and divide into two parts. Roll out each to a rectangular area of approximately 8 in × 12 in (20 cm × 30 cm) and spread with soft butter. Mix sugar and cinnamon in a small bowl and sprinkle on the surface generously.

4. Roll the dough from the length side with a sharp knife and cut into 1 in (2.5 cm) thick slices. Place the rolls of dough at a distance of 5 cm on the baking sheet and cover with a kitchen towel. Let the cinnamon buns rise for 30 minutes. Preheat the oven to 480 °F (250 °C) on the baking setting. Whisk the egg and milk, spread onto the cinnamon buns and sprinkle bake in the oven for 5—7 minutes. Put the buns along with baking paper on a wire rack to cool down.

Ticket to Sweden, please! Have you ever been there? With Michel, Lotta, and Karlsson on the roof? I was. Well, almost! Thanks to Astrid Lindgren I was quite often as a child on the way with Bullerbü and Co among the scent of cinnamon rolls ... Hach, pure Sweden!

TIP
You can bake the cinnamon buns in
mini muffin pan and serve it. If
you like them sweeter, make icing
from 1 cup (250 g) powdered sugar
and 3-4 tablespoons of water
and drizzle over the buns right
before serving. You can also put
the buns on wooden skewers.

Old cans can be perfectly remod-
eled as gift packaging. Simply
remove the paper and sharp edges,
cleanse well and paint with
chalkboard paint from the hard-
ware store. Allow to dry overnight and label with chalk.

DONUT CAKE POPS

MAKES 30-35

Dough: 1 chocolate cake ⟹ 15   cream ⟹ 12

Glaze: 2 1/2 cups (600 g) Peanut Butter Candy Melts ⟹ 140   2—3 tablespoons vegetable fat shortening   1/4 cup 3 tablespoon (100 g) white cake frosting (or white candy melts) ⟹ 140 with 2—3 tablespoon vegetable fat   sugar beads ⟹ 141

Also: 1 skewer   Styrofoam block 12 in × 20 in × 4 in (30 cm × 50 cm × 10 cm)   Ball modeling tool ⟹ 141
35 lollipop sticks ⟹ 141

1. According to the basic recipe from page 15, bake a chocolate cake and mix the ingredients for the cream. Form 30—35 cake balls. Here imprint a depression in the balls on one side with the ball modeling tool. Let the balls rest for about 15 minutes. Since the cake pops are placed to dry in a Styrofoam block, drill about 35 holes in the Styrofoam block with a skewer.

2. Affix the lollipop sticks to the balls according to the recipe. Glaze the cake donuts with peanut butter candy melts and allow to dry completely intact - preferably plugged into the Styrofoam block. Also melt the white cake frosting and spread with a small spoon on the front of the donuts. Sprinkle sugar pearls on the white glaze while still wet and lay the pops to dry on a piece of baking paper.

Hot dogs and burgers were taste-tested extensively in New York, but I somehow did not have donuts at the time. I only recently discovered my love for these sugar rings and that they can even be eaten for breakfast, although they must be acquired on location. How do I now pass the time until I come back to NY? I sit in the sunshine in the garden, drink the best cappuccino in the city (and by Mr. K), and nibble on a damn delicious donut on a stick.

VANILLA CUPCAKES

MAKES 12

Dough: 1/2 cup (120 ml) milk   1/4 cup 1 tablespoon (60 g) butter   3/4 cup 2 teaspoon (130 g) sugar   3 eggs   1 teaspoon vanilla extract ⇨ 141   grated zest of ½ untreated lemon   2 cups (200 g) flour   1 1/2 teaspoon baking powder   1 pinch of salt

Cream: 1/2 cup 1 tablespoon (125 g) butter (room temperature)   1 cup 2 tablespoon (250 g) powdered sugar   1 pinch salt   1/2 teaspoon vanilla extract   1 teaspoon cream   1 pinch of red food coloring ⇨ 141   pink sugar pearls ⇨ 141

Also: 12-muffin tin   12 paper cupcake holders pastry bag with star tip ⇨ 141

1. Preheat the oven to 360 °F (180 °C) on the baking setting and fill the muffin tin with paper cupcake holders. Warm milk and butter in a small saucepan until the butter has completely dissolved. Set aside to cool down. Stir eggs, sugar and vanilla extract until creamy with an electric whisk and add the butter mixture.

2. Add lemon zest, flour, baking powder and salt to the liquid ingredients and stir until no more clumps are visible. Fill the cupcake holders two-thirds with batter and bake for 18—20 minutes on the middle rack in the oven. Remove the cupcakes from the muffin tin and set to cool down on a wire rack.

3. For the cream stir the butter until creamy. Sieve the powdered sugar and add, beat both at least 5 minutes with the electric whisk. Dissolve the salt in the vanilla extract and add the cream to the butter mixture. Again stir well and color with red food coloring. Fill the butter cream into a pastry bag with a star tip, decorate the cooled cupcakes and sprinkle the sugar pearls on top.

I'm going on strike! Imagine standing in the kitchen all morning, baking for your life, and the photographer puts the model in his mouth without permission before he snapped a picture of it on his camera. The purest cupcake sabotage.

Well, I can understand it, yes. Vanilla and vanilla doesn't sound so exciting at first, but the pure smell of this cupcake is seduction par excellence. Anyway, a true con artist we have here. Just in pink ribbons with windmills for the girls and sometimes in blue polka dots with light blue buttercream for the boys. Simply replace the mold, sugar pearls and food coloring.

TIP

For the windmills you need paper
squares, lollipop sticks 4 in
(10 cm), patterned paper (⇨
140) and tape. Cut diagonally
from the corners to the middle
of the square and attach with
brads. Carefully place each second corner on the center of the
square and secure with brads.
Attach the lollipop stick with a
piece of tape to the back of the
windmill.`

Favorite Recipes

Sometimes you have to go to the ends of the earth to eat the first banana cake of your life. I went there at least.

My husband bought me my first slice from a few magical Fijians after a ukelele show, and it was the perfect birthday present. The first bite of chocolate cake reveals its fruity secret and within seconds you will be catapulted into banana-chocolate paradise.

TIP

Out of two paper straws (➡141), a pretty ribbon, and colored paper tape a chic cake garland can be crafted. This cake is also quite excellent for covering with fondant. This cake should be left alone at least 1 hour after decorating, so the ganache is slightly firmer and covered with fondant as on page 110.

Chocolate Banana Cake
Makes 1 cake, 12-16 slices

Ganache: 2 2/3 cup (600 g) whole milk couverture   1 3/4 cup (400 g) cream

Dough: 1 cup 2 tablespoon (250 g) sugar   1 cup 2 tablespoon (250 g) butter (room temperature)   4 eggs   1 1/3 cup (300 g) flour   3 teaspoon cocoa powder   1 packet baking powder   1 teaspoon baking soda   1 teaspoon ground cinnamon   3 ripe bananas   butter for the mold

Also: 2 springform pans (diameter 7 or 8 in [18 or 20 cm])

1. Chop the couverture into small pieces with a large knife. Boil the cream in a small saucepan on the stove. Pull the pan from the heat, sprinkle in the pieces of chocolate, let stand for 2—3 minutes and then stir with a spoon. Once the chocolate is completely melted, homogenize the ganache with a blender. Cover the bowl with plastic wrap and let rest in a cool place overnight. Ideally, keep at a temperature of about 57—60 °F (14—16 °C). Whoever doesn't have a basement should keep the ganache in the refrigerator and take it out about 1 hour before processing.

2. Preheat the oven to 320 °F (160 °C) on the baking setting. Grease 2 springform pans (diameter 7 or 8 in [18 or 20 cm]). Stir sugar, butter and eggs in a large bowl until creamy. Sieve flour, cocoa, baking powder, baking soda and cinnamon and mix well with the butter mixture. Gently stir the banana purée into the batter.

3. Fill the dough into the molds. Bake in preheated oven for 40—60 minutes. Use the toothpick test to see whether the cake is fully baked. Remove the cake from the oven, leave to rest on the mold only about 20 minutes and then take out. Let cool down completely intact on a wire rack.

4. Beat the ganache (room temperature) with the electric whisk just before brushing. Caution! Not too long, otherwise it may happen that it coagulates, similar to the whipped cream.

5. Cut the two cakes horizontally and spread only the upper surfaces of the cake layers thinly with the ganache. Lay the halves on top of each other. Spread the rest of the ganache onto the whole cake. Keeps at least 2—3 days after preparation.

Macadamia Crumble with Blackberries

Makes 4 glasses

....

Compote: 1 unwaxed lemon   1/4 cup 1 tablespoon (70 g) sugared jam   1 pinch ground cinnamon   3 cup (300 g) blackberries

Streusel: 1/4 cup 1 tablespoon (75 g) flour   1/4 cup 1 tablespoon (75 g) brown sugar   2 tablespoon (30 g) butter (cold)
2 tablespoon (30 g) salted macadamia nuts

Cream: 2/3 cup (150 g) mascarpone   3/4 cup (170 g) cream   1/4 cup 1 tablespoon (70 g) blackberry confiture   powdered sugar for dusting

Also: 4 glasses with lids (a 1 cup [230 ml]) ⟹ 140

....

1. Preheat the oven to 360 °F (180 °C) on the baking setting. Cover a baking sheet with parchment paper. Wash the lemon with hot water and pat dry. Peel and squeeze out the juice. Boil sugar, lemon juice and cinnamon, add 2 cup (200 g) of blackberries and lemon rind; continue cooking for 3 minutes. Mash the berries with a fork. Distribute the compote into the glasses and chill without covering.

2. For the streusel, finely chop flour, brown sugar, butter and nuts in a food processor. Sprinkle the mixture onto the baking sheet and bake for 15 to 20 minutes in the oven. Let cool down on the baking sheet.

3. Beat mascarpone, cream and jam until stiff with the electric whisk. Pour the cream into a pastry bag (or plastic bag with the tip cut off) and alternately layer with the streusel over the blackberry compote. Garnish with remaining berries and sprinkle with powdered sugar.

As soon as the first sun rays warm the backyard to more than 60 °F (15 °C) at house K. the teak furniture is scrubbed and the kettle grill pulled out of the garage. The man with the tongs (Mr. K.) will try from now until early September to operate the grill to perfection. I will be careful not to take away his place at the grill, but rather prepare a dessert from blackberry compote. With crumbs and cream.

For 5-6 Verry-Berry lollies you need 75 grams of candies with a berry flavor (e.g. Ricola Mixed Berry) and 5-6 wooden skewers. Preheat the oven to 440 °F (225 °C). Cover a baking sheet with an oven-safe silicone baking mat. Grind the candies to a fine powder in the food processor. Place a heart shaped cookie cutter on the silicone baking mat and sprinkle the candy powder into the cookie cutter using a sieve. The layer of powder should be 1.5-2 mm thick. Remove the powder that was sprinkled outside of the cutter with a brush. In this way, distrubute 5-6 hearts on the sheet and put a wooden skewer on the tips of the heart of each. Heat the hearts on the top rack in the oven for about 20 seconds until the powder has melted completely. Let cool on the silicone mat and carefully remove.

Flying Mushroom Cake Pops

Makes 30-35

....

Dough: 1 chocolate cake ⟹ 15   cream ⟹ 12

Glaze: 2 3/4 cup (600 g) white cake icing (or white candy melts with 2—3 tablespoons vegetable fat) ⟹ 140
1 1/3 cup (300 g) red Candy Melts with 2—3 tablespoon vegetable fat ⟹ 140   white sugar pearls ⟹ 141

Dough: 1 skewer   Styrofoam block 12 in × 20 in × 4 in (30 cm × 50 cm × 10 cm) ⟹ 141   circular cookie cutters (diameter 1 inch (2.5 cm))
35 lollipop sticks ⟹ 141

....

1. According to the basic recipe from page 15 bake a chocolate cake and mix the ingredients for the cream. Form 30—35 cake mushrooms, using a circular cookie cutter to help and let the dough chill about 15 minutes. Since the cake pops are placed to dry in a Styrofoam block, drill about 35 holes in the block with a skewer.

2. Affix the lollipop sticks to the cake pops according to the basic recipe. For glazing, first dunk the cake fungi in the white glaze and let harden completely while plugged in the Styrofoam block. You can speed up the process by briefly putting the pops in the refrigerator.

3. Dip only the tops of the mushrooms — later the umbrellas of the mushrooms — into the red candy melts, let dry a little and then put into the Styrofoam block to dry fully. Wait another 2—3 minutes until the glaze is slightly dry, but still shines and decorate with white sugar pearls.

Recently, while I was perusing a blog posting online in search of red-and-white-dotted things, I found something that made my mouth drop. A whole house was being constructed in this style. Boards, wallpaper, mugs, plates, linen and sheets, garlands, pillow cases, sofas and armchairs, table tops, baking molds and cookie jars — it's all here. If I wanted to, I could even dress myself in this flashy style. Blouses, shoes, bags, socks, and a gorgeous swimsuit I discovered as well. I suppose the trigger for this polka dot mania was these little guys, who incidentally also act as lucky charms.

Berry Crumb Cake Delight

Makes 1 cake, 12-16 slices

....

Dough: 1/2 cup 1 tablespoon (125 g) butter (room temperature)   2 eggs   1/2 cup 1 tablespoon (125 g) sugar   1 1/3 cup (300 g) flour
1/2 packet baking powder   1 cup 2 tablespoon (250 g) of berries (such as raspberries, blackberries, blueberries - or just a mixed variety)

Streusel: 1/2 cup 1 tablespoon (125 g) butter (room temperature)   7 tablespoon (100 g) sugar   1 1/2 cup (150 g) flour

Also: 1 springform pan 10 in (26 cm)   whipped cream for serving

....

1. For the dough stir butter and sugar until frothy. Gradually add eggs, flour and baking powder and chill the dough for 1 hour.

2. Gather all the ingredients for the streusel in a bowl, knead and crumble with your hands. Also chill for 1 hour.

3. Meanwhile, wash the berries (raspberries just picked) and pat dry. Cover the springform pan with parchment paper. Preheat the oven to 430 °F (220 °C) on the baking setting.

4. If the dough is too soft, add a little flour. Spread out the dough gently in the mold with your hands and press upward on the sides about 2 inches so that a small edge is created. Arrange the berries on the dough and sprinkle the crumbs on top. Bake the cake in the oven for about 40 minutes. Let cool down, remove from the mold and serve with whipped cream.

I was amazed when the wife of a baker got this little cheat sheet. After much eyelash batting and very sweet requests I finally got my hands on the recipe for these INCREDIBLY delicious cakes. What is the secret ingredient? Where does this special taste come from? Maybe I had different perceptions for the atmosphere of the enchanted castle garden of this baker's wife. The buttery caramel crumble, between berries and fresh whipped cream. All this on a cake fork? I can tell you it's a crumbly berry dream! Tastes just as good at home, incidentally, as in the castle garden. ALSO very tasty on its own is the combination of apple and raspberries. Mmm ...

Cupcake Pops

Makes 15-20

Dough: 1 chocolate cake ⟹ 15   cream ⟹ 12

Icing: 1 1/3 cup (300 g) dark cake frosting   1 3/4 cup (400 g) of white cake icing (or white candy melts with 2—3 tablespoons vegetable fat) ⟹ 140   Mini Smarties sugar pearls ⟹ 141

Also: 1 skewer   Styrofoam block 12 in × 20 in × 4 in (30 cm × 50 cm × 10 cm) ⟹ 141   flower-shaped cookie cutter 1.4 in (3.5 cm) ⟹ 140   20 lollipop sticks ⟹ 141

1. Bake a chocolate cake (⟹15) and mix with the ingredients for the cream. Mold 15—20 cake balls with a 1.4 in (3.5 cm) diameter - the balls are as large as those of the basic recipe. Place the balls for about 15 minutes in the refrigerator. Since the cake pops are placed to dry in a Styrofoam block, drill about 35 holes in the Styrofoam block with a skewer.

2. Now form the balls into cylinders and carefully stick halfway with the cookie cutter. Maybe just print the cupcake bottoms on the countertop and then remove the cookie cutter. Place the dough again 10—20 minutes in the refrigerator.

3. Now the lollipop sticks are used. In order for these to hold better, dip them into the glaze and then stick into the cupcake. Melt the dark glaze and dip the lower part of the cupcake up to halfway. Let dry on the Styrofoam block.

4. Once the dark glaze is completely hardened, next comes the white glaze. Melt this as well (if you use Candy Melts, then give 1—2 tablespoons vegetable fat prior) and dip the top half of the cupcakes into the glaze upside down. Sprinkle with sugar pearls and Smarties while the icing is still somewhat wet.

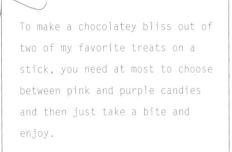

To make a chocolatey bliss out of two of my favorite treats on a stick, you need at most to choose between pink and purple candies and then just take a bite and enjoy.

Chocolate Strawberry Cupcakes

Makes 12

....

Dough: 1/4 cup 1 tablespoon (75 g) butter   1/2 teaspoon vanilla extract ⇒ 141   1 cup 1 tablespoon (250 g) flour 1/4 cup (50 g) cocoa powder   1 teaspoon baking powder   1 teaspoon baking soda   1 cup (210 g) sugar   2/3 cup (150 ml) buttermilk   1 tablespoon (100 ml) whole milk   1 egg

Cream: 7/8 cup (200 g) strawberries (plus 3.5 tablespoon (50 g) for garnishing)   5 egg whites   3/4 cup 1 teaspoon (175 g) sugar 7/8 cup (200 g) butter (room temperature)

Also: 12-muffin tin   12 paper cupcake holders pastry bag with a star tip ⇒ 141

....

1. Preheat the oven to 350 °F (175 °C) on the baking setting. Stuff the muffin tin with twelve paper cupcake holders. Melt butter and vanilla extract in a small saucepan over a low temperature and set aside to cool down.

2. Sieve flour, cocoa powder and baking powder into a large bowl. Add baking soda and sugar. Whisk together buttermilk, milk and egg in another bowl. Gradually add the butter and the milk mixture to the dry ingredients and stir everything well. Fill the cupcake holders to two-thirds and bake 17—20 minutes in the oven. Conduct a toothpick test!

3. Wash, hull, and pat dry the strawberries. Purée 7/8 cup (200 g) of berries with a blender and pass through a fine sieve. Put aside the collected purée.

4. Beat the egg whites with sugar in a glass bowl in a water bath with a whisk. Very important is that the bowl does not touch the water, otherwise the egg whites could coagulate. Heat the mixture to 150 °F (65 °C) (not hot!) and stir until the sugar has completely dissolved, which takes about 5 minutes. Remove the bowl from the water bath.

When I think of strawberries and chocolate, a very specific chocolate bar comes to mind that I was regularly eating for a short while about 17 years ago. In the commercial a young man gives his lady a whole refrigerator full of chocolate bars. Mr. K. (back then still no gentleman) did the same. Well, it was half a fridge full, but I admit, it impressed the 15-year-old girl with the strawberry-chocolate appetite very much. You can imagine that the butterflies in my stomach associated with this strawberry-chocolate cupcake definitely began to flutter.

5. Beat the egg white mixture for about 10 minutes with a whisk until it is very stiff and cold. Gradually add the softened butter in small pieces and work in well. If they do not connect with the protein mass, you can put the bowl into the water bath for a few seconds. If the mixture is too viscous, set in the refrigerator for a few minutes. Sometimes it happens that the mixture looks a little curdled shortly after adding the butter. This is quite normal. After a few minutes, a smooth cream forms from it.

6. Gently stir in 2/3 cup (150 g) strawberry purée and again work in well. Fill butter cream into a pastry bag with a star tip and decorate the cupcakes with it. If no pastry bags are available, you can spread the cream with a broad knife on the cupcake. Cut the remaining strawberries into slices. Spoon a little of the remaining purée over the cupcakes and then decorate with one or two strawberry slices.

Mini Poppy Bundt Cakes with Egg Nog

Makes 24

Small Bundt cakes for the big ones. One in each basket, two in the hand, and three left over? This recipe also guarantees you won't get poppy seeds stuck between your teeth anymore.

TIP
If the minis are not plastered immediately and on the spot, they can be very nicely decorated, such as with a small flag. For this you need a toothpick, a ribbon or a piece of cloth, and possibly some glue. Also great is a flag made of greaseproof paper with a fancy stamp. This can be cut with zig zag scissors.

Dough: 1/2 cup (110 g) butter (room temperature)   6 tablespoon 1 teaspoon (90 g) powdered sugar   1 vanilla pod   3 tablespoon (45 g) flour   6 tablespoon 1 teaspoon (90 g) semolina   2 eggs   2 tablespoons egg nog   1 pinch salt   juice and zest of 1/2 untreated lemon   2 tablespoon 2 teaspoon (35 g) baking finished poppy seeds   butter and flour for the mold

Also: 24 mini Bundt cake mold (indents 1 3/4 in (4.3 cm), 2/3 in (1.5 cm)) ⟹ 141

1. Preheat the oven to 410 °F on the baking setting. Grease the mold and sprinkle with flour. Put the butter in a small saucepan and sieve the powdered sugar into it. Heat both on the stove until the butter has completely dissolved. Stir well with a whisk and set aside.

2. Cut the vanilla pod lengthwise and scrape out the seeds. Sieve the flour into a bowl and mix with the semolina. Put in the eggs and beat with an electric whisk. Add the cooled butter mixture, egg nog, salt, lemon zest and 1 teaspoon lemon juice as well as poppy seeds and work everything into a homogeneous dough.

3. Fill the dough into a pastry bag (or a plastic bag with the tip cut off) and pour into the mini Bundt cake mold — these should be filled to the brim. Bake in the lower third of the oven for about 15 minutes. Conduct the toothpick test!

As a souvenir simply place in a basket ⟹140 and bind a bow of lace around them.

Apple Whoopie Pies with Cinnamon Cream

Makes 14-16

Dough: 1 cup 3 tablespoon (240 g) flour   1 teaspoon ground cinnamon   1 teaspoon baking powder   1/2 teaspoon baking soda
1/2 cup (115 g) butter (room temperature)   1 egg   1/2 teaspoon vanilla extract ⇒ 141   (225 g) apple sauce,   butter and flour for the mold

Cream: 2/3 cup (150 g) cream cheese (room temperature)   2 tablespoon (30 g) butter (room temperature)   2 cups (450 g) powdered sugar
1/2—1 teaspoon vanilla extract ⇒ 141

Also: 12-muffin tin (or whoopie pie mold ⇒ 141)

1. Preheat the oven to 360 °F (180 °C) on the baking setting. Sieve flour, cinnamon, baking powder and baking soda in a bowl and mix. In another bowl stir butter and sugar until creamy. Add egg and vanilla extract. Now gradually add the flour mixture alternately with the apple-sauce to the butter-sugar-egg mixture and stir well. Let the dough cool for about 30 minutes.

2. In order for the whoopie pie halves to maintain their shapes during the baking process, I place them in cupcake molds (or a whoopie pie baking pan). For this grease the wells and sprinkle with flour. Place about 1 1/2 tsp dough into each well and bake for 12—14 minutes. Let cool completely on a grid and loosen from the mold.

3. Stir cream cheese and butter until creamy. Sift powdered sugar and add gradually to the cream cheese mix. Season with cinnamon and vanilla extract. Let the filling cool at least 30 minutes. Fill the whoopie pies with the cream as described on page 56.

Apples and cinnamon? A love story of the most magical kind, I might well say. With that a cream that lets the heart leap higher. But anyone who thinks this combination fits only the colder seasons has been hugely mistaken, because when the pies are served slightly chilled they are quite outstanding at a summer picnic.

TIP
A perfect combination does not take much fuss and bother. A little candle, a ribbon, and you have a small surprise cake that fits perfectly in every picnic basket.

Dough: 1 cup 3 tablespoon (240 g) flour   1 teaspoon ground cinnamon   1 teaspoon baking powder   1/2 teaspoon baking soda   1/2 cup (115 g) butter (room temperature)   1 egg   1/2 teaspoon vanilla extract ⟹ 141   (225 g) apple sauce,   butter and flour for the mold

Cream: 2/3 cup (150 g) cream cheese (room temperature)   2 tablespoon (30 g) butter (room temperature)   2 cups (450 g) powdered sugar   1/2—1 teaspoon vanilla extract ⟹ 141

Also: 12-muffin tin (or whoopie pie mold ⟹ 141)

1. Preheat the oven to 360 °F (180 °C) on the baking setting. Sieve flour, cinnamon, baking powder and baking soda in a bowl and mix. In another bowl stir butter and sugar until creamy. Add egg and vanilla extract. Now gradually add the flour mixture alternately with the apple-sauce to the butter-sugar-egg mixture and stir well. Let the dough cool for about 30 minutes.

2. In order for the whoopie pie halves to maintain their shapes during the baking process, I place them in cupcake molds (or a whoopie pie baking pan). For this grease the wells and sprinkle with flour. Place about 1 1/2 tsp dough into each well and bake for 12—14 minutes. Let cool completely on a grid and loosen from the mold.

3. Stir cream cheese and butter until creamy. Sift powdered sugar and add gradually to the cream cheese mix. Season with cinnamon and vanilla extract. Let the filling cool at least 30 minutes. Fill the whoopie pies with the cream as described on page 56.

TIP
So that everyone is able to find
his or her own cup right away,
you can attach the picnick-
ers' little name tags to their
straws.

Blueberry Galettes
Makes 12-14

....

Dough: 1/2 cup 1/2 tablespoon (120 g) flour plus flour for the countertop   1/4 teaspoon baking powder   1 pinch salt   1/4 cup 1 tablespoon (70 g) cold butter   1/2 cup (110 g) cream cheese   1 tablespoon cold water

Filling: 14 tablespoon (200 g) blueberries (fresh or frozen)   1 lemon   3 tablespoons jam   1 1/2 tablespoons cornstarch 2 tablespoons honey   1/2 teaspoon ground cinnamon   1 pinch ground nutmeg   1 pinch ground cloves   1 egg yolk   3 tablespoons sugar

Also: cookie cutter (diameter 2 3/4 in (7 cm)) ⟹ 140

....

1. Sieve flour and baking powder in a bowl. Add salt, butter and cream cheese and stir well. Pour in 2 tablespoons of cold water and apple cider vinegar. Knead for about 2 minutes, until a smooth dough is created. Flatten the dough, wrap in cling film and place in the refrigerator for about 30 minutes.

2. Meanwhile, wash the blueberries and pat dry. Squeeze the lemon. Stir lemon juice, sugar, corn starch, honey and spices in a small bowl and gently dump in the blueberries. Preheat the oven to 430 °F (220 °C) on the baking setting. Cover a baking sheet with parchment paper.

3. Place a layer of plastic wrap on the counter and sprinkle with flour. Place the dough on the foil and sprinkle with flour again. Lay down a second layer of plastic wrap and roll it to about 1/4 in (5 mm) thick. Cut out circles. Knead the remaining dough again, roll out and repeat the process. Place the stack of dough circles on a baking sheet. Whisk the egg yolk with 2 tablespoons of water and brush the cookies with it.

Blueberries are definitely among my favorite fruits. This is probably because the most beautiful memories of my childhood are connected with them. Every year my sister and I were packed in the car with a couple of small plastic buckets and a picnic blanket, and then the whole family went into the fields of blueberries. The place where blueberries grow in abundance is still a well-kept family secret. In these cookies, the small blue fruits have a very nice effect.

TIP
The blueberries can be replaced by blackberries or raspberries. Also chopped nectarines taste great.

4. Add 2 teaspoons of the filling into the center of each dough circle. Follow the edge around halfway, so that a small pocket is produced and there is still a small opening in the middle. Brush the pocket again with the egg mixture and sprinkle with the sugar. Bake the galettes for 11—13 minutes in a hot oven until they are golden brown. Let cool down and serve.

PICNIC TIP
Do you want to take the galettes and eat on the go? Nothing easier than using the blueberry packaging. Remove all stickers from the package and then embellish. For example, with a strip of greaseproof paper and a chic ribbon.

Blondie Sandwiches with Amaretto and Walnuts

Probably the most dangerous temptation since white chocolate. Blondie doesn't take after his more well-known brother (the brownie). A juicy piece of the blondie will capture the hearts of your loved ones in no time.

TIP

To go, or for parties, a blondie sandwich is also wonderfully packaged in a gift box. Craft a fancy design from a paper straw, a piece of tape, and a piece of cardboard paper.

Makes 12

1/2 cup 1 tablespoon (130 g) butter   3/4 cup 3 tablespoon (190 g) brown sugar   1 tablespoon honey   3 tablespoon amaretto
1 3/4 cup (220 g) flour   1/4 teaspoon baking powder   1/4 teaspoon baking soda   1 pinch salt   1 egg   1/2 cup (70 g) cashew nuts
3 1/2 tablespoon (50 g) white couverture vanilla butter cream ⇨ 78   Butter for the mold

Also: 1 baking pan 9 in × 9 in (23 cm × 23 cm)

1. Preheat the oven to 375 °F (190 °C) on the baking setting. Grease the baking pan and sprinkle with flour. Heat the butter, sugar, honey and amaretto in a small saucepan on the stove until the sugar has completely dissolved. Set aside to cool down.

2. Place the flour, baking powder, baking soda and salt and stir into a mixing bowl. Add the butter mixture and the egg and beat with the electric whisk until creamy. Chop nuts and couverture into small pieces with a large knife and gently stir into the dough. Pour the batter into the tin and bake for 25—30 minutes in the oven. Let the blondie cool down in the mold at least 30 minutes and then place on a piece of baking paper.

3. Meanwhile prepare the butter cream. Stir the butter for this with the electric whisk until creamy, sieve and add the powdered sugar and mix everything for at least 5 minutes with the electric whisk. Dissolve salt in the vanilla extract and with the cream add to the butter mixture. Again, stir well and color with blue food coloring. Cut out hearts from the entire cake and brush half with the vanilla butter cream. Lay the other hearts on top and press together carefully.

Up! Cake Pops
Makes 30-35

....

Balloons: 1/4 cup (60 g) gum paste ⇒ 110   1/4 cup (60 g) fondant ⇒ 140   food coloring 141   thin, white floral wire ⇒ 140

Dough: 1 red velvet cake ⇒ 14   cream ⇒ 12

Icing: 2 1/2 cup 1 tablespoon (600 g) white cake icing (or white Candy Melts ⇒ 140 with 2—3 tablespoons vegetable fat)

Also: vegetable fat for your hands   1 skewer   Styrofoam block 12 in × 20 in × 4 in (30 cm × 50 cm × 10 cm) ⇒ 141
35 lollipop sticks ⇒ 141

....

Do you know this movie, in which one of the most enchanting love stories of all time is told within the first few minutes? It is about oodles of balloons, a boy scout, and of course, the big, big love. And then it may be that Mrs. K (perhaps me) bursts into tears at the same spot every time she sees the movie. Here is my declaration of love to this movie.

Tip
For the party table fill a sundae cup made of cardboard (⇒ 140) with mini-marshmallows and put cake pops into it.

1. For the balloons knead the gum paste and fondant together. For this purpose grease your hands with some vegetable fat so that the mass does not stick to your fingers. Color the mixture to suit your mood. Take away small pieces and shape balloons.

2. Snip about 2 in (5 cm) long pieces from the wire to wrap around a lollipop stick and carefully pull back - this results in the curved shape. Place the balloons on the wires and set aside to dry.

3. According to the basic recipe from page 14 bake a red velvet cake, mix with the ingredients for the cream. Form 30—35 cake balls and chill for 15 minutes. Since the cake pops are placed to dry in a Styrofoam block, drill about 35 holes in the Styrofoam block with a skewer. Affix the lollipop sticks to the balls according to the basic recipe.

4. Glaze the cake balls and put to dry in the Styrofoam block. Stick the balloons into the cake pops. It is best if the icing is not quite hardened.

Little Cloud Cookies

Makes 20

....

Dough: 1/2 amount favorite sugar cookie dough ⟹ 18

Glaze: 1/2 amount of egg white spray glaze or meringue powder icing ⟹ 21

Also: 2 cloud cookie cutters (diameter 1 3/4 in and 2.5 in (4.5 cm and 6.5 cm)) ⟹ 140 20   Lollipop sticks
Pastry bag with round tip ⟹ 141   Toothpicks

....

1. According to the basic recipe from page 18 to prepare and roll out half the dough 6 mm thick. Cut out 10 small and 10 large clouds and insert the lollipop sticks according to the instructions on page 19. Bake the cookies for 7—8 minutes in the oven and place on a grid to cool down. It is best to continue with the decorating the next day.

2. Place the cookies on a piece of baking paper to glaze. Blend half the amount of egg white spray glaze or meringue powder icing and dilute with a few drops of water until the desired consistency for spraying the sugared edges is reached (⟹ 20/21).

3. Pour a small amount of icing into a pastry bag with a round tip and squeeze a rim of sugar onto the cookie. Dilute the remaining glaze again with a few drops of water (⟹ 21) and place on the cookie. Let dry overnight on the baking paper.

They're floating quickly away. On a stick, or decorated with a few drops of sugar rain they are almost too pretty to nibble. Did you often sit in the meadow as a child, looking at the sky and discovering the craziest pictures?

My all-time favorite chocolate bar, my number one chocolate bar, my ultimate after-lunch snack. I know people who eat these bars for breakfast, have a top figure, and are eye doctors. I wonder to this day whether it was because of this successful combination of peanut, chocolate, and sugar that the study of medicine began. Because these bars supply luck and energy, it's totally understandable to me.

Homemade Snickers Bars

Makes 20-30

2 cups (440 g) whole milk couverture   2/3 cup (180 g) creamy peanut butter   1/4 cup (60 g) butter   1 cup (200 g) sugar

3 tablespoon (55 g) of condensed milk ⇨ 141   1 1/4 cup (150 g) marshmallow fluff ⇨ 141   1 teaspoon vanilla extract ⇨ 141

1 1/3 cup (200 g) salted peanuts   1 3/4 cup (400 g) caramel toffees   3 tablespoon (45 g) cream

Also: 1 baking dish 9 in × 11 in (22 cm × 28 cm)

1. Line the baking dish with plastic wrap. The candy bar is prepared in layers. For the first layer melt 1 cup (220 g) couverture and 1/3 cup (60 g) of peanut butter together in the water bath and pour into the mold. Put in the freezer for 15 minutes.

2. For the second layer, boil butter, sugar and condensed milk in a small saucepan until the sugar has completely dissolved. Add marshmallow fluff, 1/3 cup (60 g) peanut butter and vanilla extract and stir until smooth. Add peanuts and pour everything into the mold. Put the casserole dish in the freezer again for 15 minutes.

3. For the third layer melt caramel toffees and cream in a small saucepan on low heat, let cool down and spread over the peanut mass. For the last layer melt the couverture and peanut butter in a water bath and pour over the caramel layer. Put back in the freezer for 15 minutes and store in the refrigerator until shortly before consumption. How and whether you share the over-large chocolate bar is up to you.

But be careful — they're dangerously addictive!

TIP
With chalkboard paint one can do amazing things. Even paper bags can be embellished with it and after a short drying time labeled with chalk. Cut the candy bars into bite size pieces and wrap in aluminum foil. So they still look dapper, wrap in a layer of greaseproof paper with bows and place into the bag.

SPECIAL OCCASIONS

FONDANT CAKE WITH STRAWBERRY AND CHOCOLATE CREAM

MAKES 1 CAKE

Dough: 1 1/2 cup (200 g) milk chocolate or couverture   8 eggs   3/4 cup 3 tablespoon (190 g) sugar   1 1/3 cup (170 g) flour
4 teaspoons cocoa powder   2 tablespoon baking powder   3/4 cup 1 1/2 tablespoon (200 ml) sunflower oil for the mold

Ganache: 2 1/4 cup (300 g) bitter couverture   1 3/4 cup 1 tablespoon (440 g) cream

Sugar glue: 1/4 teaspoon (CMC food grade adhesive and binding material) ⟹ 140

Gum paste: 1 egg white   1 3/4 cup 2 tablespoon (225 g) powdered sugar   4 teaspoon painted CMC emulsifier pink food coloring ⟹ 141

Cream: 1 2/3 cup 1 tablespoon (400 g) cream   4 packets whip cream stabilizer   4 packets vanilla sugar   7/8 cup (200 g) cream cheese
1 1/4 cup (300 g) natural yogurt 3.5% fat   3 1/3 cup (500 g) strawberries   1/2 glass (about 1/2 cup (150 g)) smooth strawberry jam

Fondant: 3 cups 1 teaspoon (700 grams) of white rolled fondant ⟹ 141

Also: 2 springform pans (diameter 7 in [18 cm]) pie underlay made of cardboard (diameter 7—8 in [18—20 cm]) or cakeboard ⟹ 140
Turntable ⟹ 140   vegetable fat for your hands powdered sugar for the countertop rolling pin ⟹ 141   2 smoothers ⟹ 141 or cutting
board pizza cutter or small knife flower cookie cutters (3, 4 and 7 mm) ⟹ 140   ball modeling tool ⟹ 141   thin foam mat (packing
material) Teaspoon ⟹ 141 or round blister packaging

It is best if you prepare the bottom of the cake, ganache, flower paste, and sugar glue one day before serving the cake.
This has the advantage that the bottom of the cake can be cut better and not immediately absorb the cream filling.
Wrapped in cling film then waiting to be used, e.g. as a birthday cake for the best Mom in the world.

1. For the bottom of the cake, preheat the oven to 340 °F (170 °C) on the baking setting. Grease the springform pans with a little oil. Melt the chocolate in a bowl in a water bath and set aside to cool down. Stir eggs and sugar until creamy. Mix flour, cocoa and baking powder. Gradually add the oil and the flour mixtures by stirring into the sugar mass. Carefully stir in the liquid chocolate. Pour the batter into the two springform pans and bake for about 40 minutes at 340 °F (170 °C). Conduct the toothpick test! Let the bottom of the cake cool down in the mold, then loosen and let cool down completely intact on a wire rack. If you aren't until putting the bottom together until the next day, then pack in plastic wrap overnight.

2. Chop the couverture into small pieces with a large knife. Boil the cream in a small saucepan on the stove. Pull the pan from the heat, sprinkle in the pieces of chocolate, let stand for 2—3 minutes and then stir with a spoon. Once the chocolate is completely melted, homogenize the ganache with an immersion blender. Cover the bowl with plastic wrap and let rest in a cool place overnight. Ideally, keep at a temperature of about 57—60 °F (10—15 °C). Whoever doesn't have a basement should leave the ganache in the refrigerator and take it out about 1 hour before continuing.

3. For the sugar glue, fill 1/4 tsp CMC in a small, crafty screw top jar. Put some tap water in a small saucepan to boil, measure out 30 ml and pour over the CMC. Close the jar, shake well and allow the adhesive to soak in the refrigerator for 24 hours. The sugar glue keeps for about two weeks if stored.   >>>

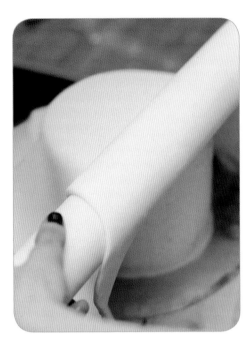

4. For the flower paste, beat the egg whites with the KitchenAid on a high setting for about 10 seconds. Sieve the powdered sugar. Take 2 tablespoons of it and put aside. The kitchen machine can run on the lowest level and you can sprinkle in the remaining sugar. Now increase the speed and let the machine run for about 2 minutes, until the mixture shines silky and soft peaks form. Slow down a little and let the CMC trickle into the powdered sugar-protein mass. Then let the machine run for a few seconds on a high setting. The mass is now fixed. Sieve the remaining powdered sugar on the countertop, put the flower paste on top, lightly grease your hands with vegetable fat and knead the powdered sugar into the mixture. Put the paste in a freezer bag, seal airtight and let stand for 24 hours in refrigerator. Before processing warm the paste to room temperature.

5. For the cream, whip the cream with 2 packets whip cream stabilizer and the vanilla sugar until stiff according to package directions. Stir cream cheese with yogurt and add in remaining cream stabilizer until smooth. Carefully pull the cream under the cream cheese mixture. Keep the mass cool until working with it again. Wash the strawberries, hull, and pat dry. Cut the berries into thin slices and set aside.

6. Cut the round dome of the bottom of the cake with a sharp knife and cut each horizontally in the middle. Cut a cake underlayer made of cardboard to the exact size of the cake 7 in (18 cm). It later allows a better transport of the cake to the cake plate. Spread a very thin layer of butter cream to the center of the turntable so that the cake does not slip. Put the cake underlayer on the turntable. Place the first layer with the cut-off side on top of the cake underlayer and spread with strawberry jam and cream. Leave at least .7 in (2 cm) from the border free, so that the filling does not fall out later over the sides and dissolve the fondant. Put on the second layer and lightly press. Brush this with cream and top with strawberries. Add on the third layer and spread as with the first layer. The fourth layer completes the cake.

7. Now beat the ganache slowly with an electric whisk until creamy. Don't stir too long, the mass will curdle. Now coat the entire cake with ganache and cool for at least 2 hours. Whoever does not like fondant ends here. The cake tastes good and bombastic now and with a small banner it is also a real eye-catcher.

8. For the fondant shell first measure the cake (height × 2 + internal diameter +1.5–2 1/3 in [4–6 cm] excess). Now clean the countertop. Even if you see no dust, believe me, there is some. Grease hands with vegetable fat, dust rolling pin and worktop with powdered sugar. Knead the fondant gradually until soft, so that later it does not tear. This may take about 30 minutes. Roll out fondant to 3mm thick. If it sticks to the work surface, use more

sugar. Place the rolled fondant on the rolling pin and then gently drape over the cake. With the smoothers (or cutting board) firmly press the fondant first at the top, and then softly on both sides of the cake. Cut the surplus of the cake's bottom layer with a pizza cutter (or sharp knife).

9. For the flowers cleanse the countertop again thoroughly, grease your hands with vegetable fat and knead the flower paste until supple. Once the paste begins to stick to your hands, lubricate quickly. Use a small portion of the paste and pack the rest in a plastic bag. (If desired, color some of the paste pink.) Roll out the flower paste 2 mm thick. Cut out one flower with the cookie cutter and carefully place it on the foam mat. Grease the ball

modeling tool on the thick tip and carefully spread outward from the center of the petals. So that the flowers are round press the teaspoon down (or another object with which to form around the flower eg the blister packaging from the toffee). Brush the flowers on the back side with a little sugar glue and attach them to the cake according to your preferences. Cool the cake 2 hours prior to serving.

WHOOPIE PIES WITH GREEN TEA AND CHERRY CREAM

MAKES 16

Dough: 3 bags of green tea   1/2 cup 1 tablespoon (125 g) butter (room temperature)   3/4 cup 1 tablespoon (165 g) sugar   1 egg   1 teaspoon vanilla extract ⟹ 141   2 1/3 cup 1 tablespoon (300 g) flour   1 teaspoon baking powder   1/2 teaspoon baking soda   1 pinch green food coloring ⟹ 141

Cream: 1 1/3 cup (300 g) sour cherries (1 glass)   3 tablespoons sugar   1 1/2 packet custard powder   1—2 tablespoon powdered sugar   1 cup 1 tablespoon (250 g) butter   16 sweet cherries for decorating powdered sugar for dusting

Also: pastry bag with rose tip ⟹ 141

1. Fill up a cup with a teabag and 1/2 cup (125 ml) of boiling water and let stand for 1 hour and wring well. Preheat the oven to 365 °F (180 °C) on the baking setting and cover two baking sheets with parchment paper. Stir butter and sugar until creamy, add egg and vanilla extract and mix well. Sieve the flour, baking powder and baking soda in a bowl and gradually add to butter mixture. Add green tea and food coloring and mix with the electric whisk until the mixture is uniformly dyed.

2. Place the dough into a pastry bag with a round tip (or a plastic bag with the tip cut off). Set walnut sized balls of dough at a distance of 2 in (5 cm) on the baking sheet and bake whoopie pies for about 12 minutes in a hot oven until golden brown. Afterwards, allow 2 minutes on the baking sheet and then carefully put on a wire rack to fully cool.

3. Measure 7/8 cup (200 ml) of cherry juice from the jar and purée the cherries. Mix the pudding powder with about 2 tablespoons of sugar. Gradually stir smooth with at least 6 tablespoons of purée. Boil the rest of the purée, remove from heat and stir the mixed powder.

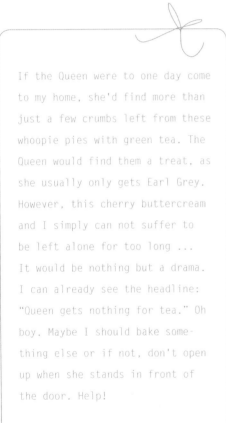

If the Queen were to one day come to my home, she'd find more than just a few crumbs left from these whoopie pies with green tea. The Queen would find them a treat, as she usually only gets Earl Grey. However, this cherry buttercream and I simply can not suffer to be left alone for too long ... It would be nothing but a drama. I can already see the headline: "Queen gets nothing for tea." Oh boy. Maybe I should bake something else or if not, don't open up when she stands in front of the door. Help!

Boil the pudding while stirring for 1 minute. Let cool down, put through a fine sieve and cover with a layer of plastic wrap to prevent a film from forming. Then let cool completely.

4. Stir in the powdered sugar with the butter until creamy for 3 minutes. Add in the cooled cherry pudding by portions, and again stir well. Fill the butter cream into a pastry bag with a rose tip or a plastic bag with the tip cut off and squeeze onto the flat side of a whoopie pie half. Also put some butter cream on another half and press together the two halves gently. On the upper surfaces also spread some butter cream, garnish with cherries and sprinkle with powdered sugar.

BIRDIE CUPCAKES

MAKES 12

....

Dough: vanilla cupcake batter ⇒ 78

Cream: vanilla cream ⇒ 78

Fondant: 2 cup 2 1/2 tablespoon (500 g) rolled fondant ⇒ 141   1 pinch pink food coloring ⇒ 141   sugar glue

Also: 12-muffin tin   12 paper cupcake holders vegetable fat for your hands rolling pin ⇒ 141   circular cookie cutters (about 6.5 cm) ⇒ 140   Smoother ⇒ 141 or cutting board

....

1. Prepare cupcakes and butter cream according to the recipe from page 78. Sprinkle the countertop with powdered sugar and grease your hands with a little vegetable fat. Softly knead the fondant with your hands until it has the desired elasticity. Of this, pack 3/4 cup (200 g) fondant in a plastic bag and set it aside.

2. Color 1 1/3 cup (300 g) fondant according to the recipe on page 128 with pink food coloring. The fondant is not used immediately, again stick in the bag so it does not dry. Sprinkle the cupcakes as on page 22 with butter cream and cover with pink fondant.

3. For the birdies sketch out on a piece of paper a small body (about 1 3/4 in × 3/4 in (4.5 cm × 2 cm)) and wings (about 1 1/8 in × 1/2 in (3 cm × 1.5 cm)) and cut out as templates. Roll out the remaining white fondant thinly, place the stencil on top and cut out with a sharp knife twelve times. Brush the underside of the birdie with some sugar glue and stick on the cupcake.

Special occasions need special cupcakes. What would a baby shower be like with birdie cupcakes? A staged reception for the new parents and an affordable little thing for the guests.

Just put greaseproof paper
onto the birdie and trace
with a pencil ...

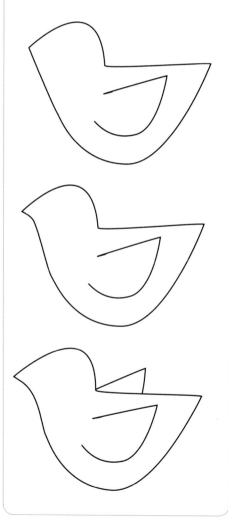

LEMON CURD MACARONS

MAKES 15–20

Dough: Macaron dough ⇨ 16   1 pinch yellow food coloring ⇨ 141

Lemon Curd: 3–4 untreated lemons   3/4 cup (155 g) sugar   3 eggs   1 pinch of salt   1/3 cup 1 teaspoon (85 g) butter

Also: 2 sterilized glasses with screw cap (1 cup [250 ml])

1. According to the basic recipe from page 16 bake yellow macarons.

2. For the lemon curd wash lemons first in hot water, dry and finely grate the peel. Of these, set aside approximately 1 tablespoon lemon zest. Squeeze the lemons and measure 1/3 cup (75 ml) of juice.

3. Warm lemon zest and lemon juice with sugar, eggs and salt in a stainless steel or glass bowl in a water bath. Attention! The bowl should not touch the water, otherwise there is a risk that the eggs will curdle. Stir gently with a rubber scraper and avoid foaming.

4. Cut the butter into small cubes. Once the sugar has completely dissolved and the mixture is thickened (this can sometimes take up to 15 minutes), gradually add the butter. The butter pieces should be completely dissolved and the cream should have a pudding-like consistency. Remove the bowl from the water bath and stir the cold mass.

Back when I mutated into a monster bride before my wedding, I agonizingly considered what you could treat the guests to at a rich champagne reception. It should be something fine, appropriate to the occasion, which also offers something for the eyes and palate. Had I only met you sooner, my dear macarons.

TIP
Use craft toothpicks, stamp letters, adhesive and resistant paper pennants.

5. To store pour the lemon curd into 2 glasses with screw caps and place in the refrigerator. There, it keeps about 10 days. Fill the chilled macarons with lemon curd and immediately serve or give away.

GHOST CAKE POPS

MAKES 30–35

Dough: 1 chocolate cake ⇨ 15   cream ⇨ 12

Icing: 2 3/4 cup (600 g) light blue Candy Melts ⇨ 140   2—3 tablespoon vegetable fat   black glitter sugar ⇨ 140
Ghosts made of sugar ⇨ 140   Yellow Mini Smarties

Also: 1 skewer   Styrofoam block 12 in × 20 in × 4 in (30 cm × 50 cm × 10 cm) ⇨ 141   35 lollipop sticks ⇨ 141

Now they're haunted too. In the semi-darkness these little ghosts can be quite creepy. These cake pops should only be presented if no scaredy-cats are present, when the moon is in the sky, when all present wear pajamas and have not brushed their teeth yet. A slumber party with your best friends would also be exactly the right opportunity.

1. According to the basic recipe from page 15 bake a chocolate cake and mix the ingredients for the cream. Form 30—35 cake balls and let sit for about 15 minutes. Since the cake pops are placed to dry in a Styrofoam block, drill about 35 holes in the Styrofoam block with a shish kebab skewer. Then attach the lollipop sticks to the balls according to the basic recipe and glaze the cake balls with light blue candy melts. Insert into the Styrofoam block to dry.

2. The decorations stick on wonderfully as long as the glaze still shines a little. For the sprinkles I hold the cake pop with one hand on the stick and turn it on its head. With the other hand I sprinkle the sugar on the bottom. The little ghosts and the moon from Mini Smarties can be put on with tweezers or with a steady hand.

When a monster bride gets married, some very strong nerves are required (especially by the future husband). Emergency baskets by the toilets, patterned napkins during the champagne reception, surprise goodie bags for kids, and a game box, a photo booth, a singer at the church, card invitations sent over from America, flower children in fancy clothes with decorated baskets, a self-made wedding candle, flower decorations with a value of a short trip to Paris, car bows, a ring pillow sewed by the world's best Mom, a DJ for the best party, and a thank you photo CD must already be prepared. (Any similarities to living persons and real actions are purely coincidental and not intentional.) Not to mention the ultimate guest gift — for example, a cookie in the shape of a wedding cake or a bridal gown.

WEDDING COOKIES

MAKES AROUND 12

Dough: favorite sugar cookie dough ⇨ 18

Glaze: 1 1/3 cup (300 g) of white fondant sugar glue ⇨ 110 or 2/3 cup (80 g) powdered sugar   1/2 amount 1 1/4 cup (200 g) of egg white spray glaze or glaze of meringue powder ⇨ 20—21

Also: wedding cake cookie cutter (about 4 in × 4.5 in (10 cm × 11.5 cm)) ⇨ 140   powdered sugar for the countertop rolling pin ⇨ 141

1. According to the basic recipe from page 18 prepare the dough and roll out as described 6 mm thick. Cut out the cookies and bake twelve cakes. Place the cookies for decorating on a piece of baking paper.

2. Grease your hands with some vegetable fat and knead the fondant until soft. Sprinkle the countertop with powdered sugar and roll out fondant to 1 mm thick. Now also cut out the fondant cakes twelve times with the cookie cutter. Brush the bottom of the fondant cakes with a little sugar glue and press on the cookies. Instead of sugar glue you can also stir 3/4 cup 1 tablespoon (80 g) of powdered sugar with a few drops of water to form a paste.

3. Meanwhile, prepare the glaze and once the fondant is connected to the cookie, pour the icing into a pastry bag with a round tip and squeeze onto the contours of the wedding cake. Allow to dry overnight and pack the cookies just before giving away.

TIP
Packaging idea for the bride-dress-cookies: Cut a piece of cardboard paper 4 × 4 in (10 × 10 cm) and stick in a cellophane bag (about 7.5 inches long (19 cm long)) and 4 1/3 in wide (11 cm wide)). Carefully put in the cookies. Fix the bottom and the cellophane on the leftover bottom side of bag with some masking tape or adhesive tape.

PARTY CUPCAKES

MAKES 12

....

Dough: vanilla cupcake batter ⟹ 78

Cream: vanilla cream ⟹ 78

Fondant: 2 cup 2 1/2 tablespoon (500 g) rolled fondant ⟹ 141   1 pinch of pink, yellow, blue and green food coloring ⟹ 141
sugar glue ⟹ 110

Also: 12—muffin tin   12 paper cupcake holders   powdered sugar for the countertop   vegetable fat for your hands   rolling pin ⟹ 141
circular cookie cutters (about 2.5 in (6.5 cm) diameter)   Smoother ⟹ 141 or cutting board

....

1. Prepare cupcakes and butter cream according to the recipe of page 78. Sprinkle the countertop with powdered sugar and grease the hands with a little vegetable fat. Knead the fondant with your hands softly until it has the desired elasticity. Of this, pack 1/3 cup (300 g) fondant in a plastic bag and set it aside.

2. For the banner of flags distribute an equal share of the remaining fondant into four large pieces and color each with pink, yellow, blue and green food coloring. Form a ball, drill a hole and use a toothpick (or small spoon) to pour in some color. Close the hole again and knead until the fondant is dyed uniformly. The fondant is not used immediately, again stick in the bag so it does not dry.

Tiny bunting in delicate pastel colors that are easily prepared? It's not for nothing that these cupcakes have swept up the category "Perfect Party" without any honest competition for the title. The highest amount of points was given in complete euphoria. Let's get this party started!

3. Roll out the colored fondant 1.5 mm thick and cut about .4 in (1 cm) wide strips. Now cut triangles with a sharp knife. The finished small pennants should be packed in a plastic bag or covered with plastic wrap until used. Spread onto the cupcakes as on page 22 and cover with butter cream and white fondant 1 1/3 cup (300 g). Brush the underside of the pennants with a little sugar glue and drape a chain on the cupcakes.

HEART CAKE POPS

MAKES 30–35

Heart: 3/4 cup 2 tablespoon (25 g) flower paste ⇨ 110   3/4 cup 2 tablespoon (25 g) fondant ⇨ 141   red food coloring ⇨ 141

Dough: 1 red velvet cake ⇨ 14   cream ⇨ 12

Glaze: 2 2/3 cup (600 g) white cake icing (or white candy melts with 2—3 tablespoons vegetable fat) ⇨ 141

Also: vegetable fat for the hands   1 skewer   1 Styrofoam block 12 in × 20 in × 4 in (30 cm × 50 cm × 10 cm) ⇨ 141   35 lollipop sticks white, thin floral wire ⇨ 140

1. For the hearts knead together flower paste and fondant. For this purpose grease your hands with some vegetable fat so that the mass does not stick to your fingers. Color the mix with food coloring. Remove small pieces and form hearts.

2. Snip the wire into about 2 in (5 cm) long pieces to wrap around a lollipop stick and carefully pull back, the result is a curved shape. Carefully press the little hearts onto the wires and set aside to dry.

3. According to the basic recipe on page 14 bake a red velvet cake, then mix the ingredients for the cream. Form 30—35 cake balls and let rest for about 15 minutes. Since the cake pops will be placed to dry in a Styrofoam block, drill about 35 holes in the Styrofoam block with a skewer. Attach the lollipop sticks according to the basic recipe for cake balls.

4. Glaze the cake balls white and let dry on the Styrofoam block. Insert the wire with the hearts into the cake pops. It's best if the icing has not quite hardened. Now you can taste love!

Love is in the air....In these enchanting cake pops an extra-large portion belongs to love. Love makes everything taste better, outdoing even the flavors of butter and chocolate. Love in surplus? I'm into it!

TIP

Stamping a piece of cardboard with "Thank You" and attaching it to the lollipop stick makes these cake pops the perfect gift for Valentine's Day or a wedding anniversary.

My heartfelt thanks

MARSHMALLOW CAKE POPS

MAKES 30-35

....

Dough: 1 chocolate cake ⟹ 15   cream ⟹ 12

Icing: 2 2/3 cup (600 g) white cake icing (or white Candy Melts ⟹ 141 with 2—3 tablespoons vegetable fat)   1 1/3 cup (300 g) of whole milk cake frosting   pink sugar pearls ⟹ 141

Also: 1 skewer   Styrofoam block 12 × 20 × 4 in (30 cm × 50 cm × 10 cm) ⟹ 141   35 lollipop sticks ⟹ 141

....

1. According to the basic recipe from page 15 bake a chocolate cake and mix the ingredients for the cream. Form 30—35 cylinders and let sit for about 15 minutes. Since the cake pops will be placed to dry in a Styrofoam block, drill about 35 holes into the block with a skewer. Affix the lollipop sticks according to the balls in the basic recipe.

2. For glazing dip the cylinders into the white icing and leave plugged into the Styrofoam block to harden completely. This you can speed up if you briefly place the pops in the refrigerator.

3. Only immerse half of the cylinders into the chocolate glaze. Wait 2-3 minutes until the glaze is slightly dry, but still shines. Put pink sugar pearls into a bowl and dip the upper half of the cylinder into them.

I have always thought that marshmallows were like licorice — you either love them or you hate them. No middle ground, not from time to time, no compromise. However, with my marshmallow cake pops it is somehow possible. They look just like marshmallows — but taste like chocolate.

TIP
Serve the cupcakes in a popcorn box (⟹ 140) and decorate with mini-marshmallows. Thus, the true marshmallow lovers get their fill and they fit nicely "instead of popcorn" with a DVD evening.

LEMON CAKE WITH LEMON CURD

MAKES 1 CAKE

Dough: 6 eggs   1 packet vanilla sugar   1 3/4 cup (350 g) sugar   1 1/2 cup (350 g) butter (room temperature)   2 untreated lemons   1 packet baking soda butter for the molds

Vanilla cream: 1 1/4 cup (290 g) butter (room temperature)   2 1/2 cup (300 g) powdered sugar   2 tablespoon (30 ml) milk 1/2 teaspoon vanilla extract ⇨ 141

Lemon curd cream: 1/4 cup 3 tablespoon (100 g) butter (room temperature)   1/2 cup (120 g) cream cheese (room temperature)   1 1/2 tablespoons (10 g) powdered sugar   1/2 cup 1 tablespoon (120 g) lemon curd ⇨ 118 or 141

Fondant: 3 cups (700 grams) white rolled fondant ⇨ 141   2 springform pans (diameter 7 in [18 cm])   Pie underlay made of cardboard or Cakeboard (diameter 8 in [18—20 cm]) ⇨ 140   Turntable ⇨ 140   Palmin soft for the hands   Powdered sugar for the work surface   Roller ⇨ 141 2 smoothers ⇨ 141 or a breakfast plate   pizza cutter or small knife   7 cooling racks ⇨ 140 or wooden skewers   7 pompoms made of paper ⇨ 141   yellow satin ribbon

1. Preheat the oven to 347 °F (175 °C) on the baking setting and grease the springform pans. Stir the eggs, vanilla, and sugar until creamy and gradually add the butter. Wash the lemons in hot water, pat dry, remove the peels, squeeze out the juice and measure out a 1/2 cup (100 ml).

2. Mix the flour with the baking powder and half of the lemon zest and stir in the lemon juice alternately with the egg mixture. Distribute the dough evenly among the molds - measure if necessary - and place the two molds in the hot oven for 50—55 minutes. To check for doneness do a toothpick test! Let the cakes stand for 10 minutes to form, then loosen and leave on a wire rack to cool down completely intact. Wait to put together the bottom of the cake until the next day, then pack in plastic wrap overnight.   >>>

"Dough is just dough!" a clever person once told me. Yes, you're correct, but you can make it a bit prettier, right? I never leave the house only in underwear. I would prefer wearing a chic summer dress on top. Maybe in yellow to match this fine cake. Oh yes, and then celebrating a garden party with Nadine and Sarah with flowers on the apple trees and so on. Without the two of them I never would have come across this wonderful recipe. Sarah invented it and Nadine has baked it dozens of times already. My humble self then had to come up with the fondant and found just the thing — TADAAA! It is the juiciest, most lemony fondant icing ever.

3. To make the vanilla cream stir the butter for at least 7 minutes until creamy. Sieve the powdered sugar and add in portions. Add milk and vanilla extract. Stir for another 5 minutes. The butter cream can be processed immediately. For the lemon curd cream, mix the cream cheese gradually with the butter using the electric whisk. Sieve in the powdered sugar. Add the lemon curd and remaining lemon zest to the cream cheese mixture and stir well.

4. Cut off the round dome cake bottoms with a sharp knife. Then cut through each cake horizontally, one time, so that four layers are formed. Cut a cake underlayer out of cardboard to the exact size of the cake (7 in [18 cm]). Later this allows a better transportation of the cake onto the serving plate. Spread a very thin layer of butter cream over the middle of the turntable (or the cardboard underlayer) so the cake does not slip when being coated. Place the cake on the turntable.

5. Place the first layer with the cut surface on top of the cake underlayer and spread a thin layer of lemon curd cream over the surface with the palette of a large knife. Leave a little less than an inch free on the edge so that the cream does not come into contact with the fondant later on. Proceed likewise with the second and third layers. Place the fourth layer with the cut surface facing down. If the cake looks uneven, straighten with a sharp knife.

6. Spread a fine layer of vanilla cream over the cake. Slowly rotate the turntable with one hand and hold the other perpendicular to the whole side of the cake with the palette knife. This quickly results in a uniformly thick layer. Place the cake in the refrigerator for 30 minutes. Then spread a second layer of vanilla cream onto the cake; if the cake layers are still visible in some spots, repeat again. Before the cake is covered with fondant, refrigerate for at least 1 hour so the butter cream will already be hardened and won't melt.

7. Distribute the fondant coating according to the basic recipe from page 112 and let the cake sit for 2 hours before slicing. With the help of some tape attach the pompoms to the wire cooling rack and into the cake at varying heights. Tie a satin ribbon around the bottommost edge of the cake.

Together, the various tiny sweets that make you happy provide for a special celebration. For example, the windmill cupcakes are an extremely good fit with the lemon cake — the result is a very extraordinary cake buffet in delicate pastel colors.

INDEX

SHOPPING GUIDE & DECORATION TIPS

Cutter for cookies: www.staedter.de

Ribbons: www.dieschoenhaberei.de
Baking Case: www.dieschoenhaberei.de
Blueberry fruit powder: www.pati-versand.de
Floral wire: www.torten-kram.eu
Petal cookie cutters: www.torten-kram.eu

Callebaut Callet: www.pati-versand.de
Cakeboard: www.torten-kram.eu
Candy Melts: www.meincupcake.de
CMC: www.pati-versand.de
Cupcake molds: www.dieschoenhaberei.de
Cupcake toppers: www.dieschoenhaberei.de or
www.meincupcake.de

Turntable: Ikea
Dulce de Leche: see caramel spread
Sundae made of cardboard: www.dieschoenhaberei.de
Ice cream cones: in the well-stocked supermarket

Fondant: www.torten kram.eu-roll

Ghosts of sugar: www.cake-pops.de
Glass, oven safe: Mason Glass: www.blueboxtree.com / en
Glitter sugar, black: www.cake-pops.de

Wedding cake cookie cutters: www.meincupcake.de
Wooden forks e.g. Papstar: www.amazon.de
Caramel spread e.g. the brand name Bonne Maman: Can be
found in well-stocked supermarkets

Ball-modeling tool: www.torten-kram.eu

Condensed milk, sweetened e.g. Nestlé,
a brand of "sugared condensed milk": well-
stocked supermarket

Food coloring, e.g. color paste of sugar
and flair www.staedter.de

Lemon curd: e.g. Chivers,
well-stocked supermarket Lollipop sticks:
www.cake-pops.de

Macadamia nut oil: www.oelmuehle-solling.de

Jam jar label: www.dieschoenhaberei.de

Vanilla Marshmallow Fluff: www.amazon.de

Meringue powder: www.meincupcake.de

Mini ring cake mold: www.staedter.de

Brad fastenings: stationery store

Paper tape (masking tape):
dawanda.com/shop/TschauTschuessi

Paper cupcake holders: www.dieschoenhaberei.de
or www.meincupcake.de

Paper bags, striped (Candy Bag):
www.dieschoenhaberei.de

Parchment paper bags: dawanda.com

Pompons: www.pompomyourlife.de

Popcorn box: www.schoenhaberei.de

Rolling pin: www.torten-kram.eu

Rosewater: pharmacy

Rose tips 16 mm: www.staedter.de

Smoother: www.torten-kram.eu

Smoothie cups: www.schoenhaberei.de

Piping bag: www.staedter.de stamp, www.bastisrike.
de, www.muji.de

Letter stamp: stamp www.muji.de

Fork:
http://de.dawanda.com/shop/karamelo-stempel

Homemade by me for you stamp:
http://de.dawanda.com/shop/bastisRIKE :
http://www.stempel-malter.de

Punches and trailer:
http://de.dawanda.com/shop/
derkleinesperling

Straws: www.dieschoenhaberei.de

Styrofoam block: www.meincupcake.de or old packing
material

Blackboard paint: DIY take away box:
www.dieschoenhaberei.de

Teaspoon: www.torten-kram.eu

Vanilla extract, for example liquid vanilla beans
extract of Taylor & Colledge: www.amazon.de or
Dr. Oetker Finesse: well-stocked supermarket

Whoopie pie-baking: www.meincupcake.de

Cloud cookie cutters: www.staedter.de

Sugar pearls: www.staedter.de

For kindly providing bakeware,
tableware, decorations and more, I
thank you very much:

ASA Selection GmbH

Rudolf-Diesel-Strasse 3

56203 Hoehr-Grenzhausen

+49 2624 1890

www.asa-selection.com

meincupcake

MeinCupcake.de

Nordring 40

50259 Pulheim

+49 2238 9595058

www.meincupcake.de

Städter GmbH

Am Kreuzweg 1

35469 Allendorf

+49 6407 4034-1000

www.staedter.de

DANI SAYS "THANKS"

I want to thank from my heart all those who have helped us in the development of this book. The pure insanity.

I thank my family and friends for the consistent support and listening at any hour of the day. Especially my mother for the supply of incredible amounts of materials to perfectly set the scene in *Little Sweets and Bakes*.

My thanks also to Marc and Petra. You have paved the way for us and our many culinary excursions. Simply the greatest friends in the world.

I thank my monster brides, because without you there would not have been a blog, and thus no book. Merci!

Thanks to Angela from the blog The Schoenhaberei for providing many wonderful things with which to beautify the baked goods. The same applies to Rike from Bastis Rike, Kathrin from Karamelo, Mi-Nu, Blueboxtree parties,

townspeople, Asa, My Cupcake.com, Monika from Tortentante.blogspot.com and Sarah of Sarah-Torten.blogspot.com for the recipes.

I say "Thank you" to all the bloggers out there who design their blogs with lots of love and who share their ideas with us. And "Thank you" to my colleagues and neighbors who have always enjoyed testing the baked goods. The "When are you going to bake again?" has always delighted me. Thank you to Markus and Karin - my bosses - for letting me take this chance.

However, no one has contributed more to the publication of this book than my editor Vanessa Herget and our graphic artist Tina Defaux. Two who have more faith in us than even ourselves. Also I thank Petra Puster, Katharina Kuenzel, and Mr. Blaschke for their enthusiastic cooperation. To Angela Thomaschik a particularly large thank you for your trust.

Without my husband Marcel I would have never tackled this project. He is responsible for the photographs on both the blog and in this book and has been my second half for already longer than half my lifetime. With a dangerous half-knowledge we started the blog about two years ago and were surprised at the positive response. I am happy and grateful for the time we are able to spend together.

MR. K SAYS "THANKS"

I would like to thank our family and friends, who for us are one and the same, for all of the love, understanding, and support without which this book would never have been created.

Thanks to my friend Marc Hillesheim, for his help in all areas of photography. Whenever I needed your help, you were there on the spot. Thank you especially for the constructive criticism of the first photos in this book. I hope I have not disappointed you.

My thanks also extend to my brother Sven, my sister-in-law Kasia and my two nephews, Matti and Gianluca, for all the encouragement during the creation of this book. Thank you for always being there when we needed you.

I would especially like to thank my parents, Gertrude and Konrad Klein, for bringing me into this world and for everything else.
Finally, I would like to thank my best friend and wife, Daniela. For the

many adventures that I've been able to experience with you, and without whom this one would never have been possible. Without you my life would be much more boring. I love you - ALWAYS.

COPYRIGHT PAGE

TEXTS AND RECIPES Daniela Klein, Kerpen

www.klitzeklein.wordpress.com

PHOTOGRAPHY Marcel Klein, Kerpen

EDITORIAL Vanessa Herget, Neustadt / Wine Road Petra Puster, Niederpocking

DESIGN, MANUFACTURE AND ASSEMBLY Tina Defaux Neustadt / Wine Road

REPRODUCTION Blaschke vision, free court

PRINTING AND PROCESSING Finidr, sro, Cesky Tesin